New Day

Edited by **Gordon Giles**

September–December 2025

 Ministries

15 The Chambers, Vineyard,
Abingdon OX14 3FE
+44 (0)1865 319700 | brf.org.uk

Bible Reading Fellowship is a charity (233280) and company limited by guarantee (301324), registered in England and Wales

EU Authorised Representative: Easy Access System Europe –
Mustamäe tee 50, 10621 Tallinn, Estonia, **gpsr.requests@easproject.com**

ISBN 978 1 80039 358 5

Distributed in Australia by:
MediaCom Education Inc, PO Box 610, Unley, SA 5061
Tel: 1 800 811 311 | admin@mediacom.org.au

Distributed in New Zealand by:
Scripture Union Wholesale, PO Box 760, Wellington 6140
Tel: 04 385 0421 | suwholesale@clear.net.nz

Acknowledgements
Scripture quotations marked with the following abbreviations are taken from the version shown. Where no abbreviation is given, the quotation is taken from the same version as the headline reference. NRSV: the New Revised Standard Version Updated Edition. Copyright © 2021 National Council of Churches of Christ in the United States of America. Used by permission. All rights reserved worldwide. NIV: The Holy Bible, New International Version, Anglicised edition, copyright © 1979, 1984, 2011 by Biblica. Used by permission of Hodder & Stoughton Publishers, an Hachette UK company. All rights reserved. 'NIV' is a registered trademark of Biblica. UK trademark number 1448790. NLT: The Holy Bible, New Living Translation, copyright © 1996, 2004, 2007, 2013. Used by permission of Tyndale House Publishers, Inc., Carol Stream, Illinois 60188. All rights reserved. NEB: the New English Bible copyright © Cambridge University Press and Oxford University Press 1961, 1970. All rights reserved. GNT: the Good News Bible published by The Bible Societies/HarperCollins Publishers Ltd, UK © American Bible Society 1966, 1971, 1976, 1992, used with permission.

The quotation from the Authorised Version of the Bible (The King James Bible), the rights in which are vested in the Crown, is reproduced by permission of the Crown's Patentee, Cambridge University Press. The scripture quotation from *The Message* is copyright © 1993, 1994, 1995, 1996, 2000, 2001, 2002 by Eugene H. Peterson. Used by permission of NavPress. All rights reserved. Represented by Tyndale House Publishers, Inc.

A catalogue record for this book is available from the British Library

Printed and bound in the UK by Zenith Media NP4 0DQ

Suggestions for using *New Daylight*

Find a regular time and place, if possible, where you can read and pray undisturbed. Before you begin, take time to be still and perhaps use the prayer of BRF Ministries on page 6. Then read the Bible passage slowly (try reading it aloud if you find it over-familiar), followed by the comment. You can also use *New Daylight* for group study and discussion, if you prefer.

The prayer or point for reflection can be a starting point for your own meditation and prayer. Many people like to keep a journal to record their thoughts about a Bible passage and items for prayer. In *New Daylight* we also note the Sundays and some special festivals from the church calendar, to keep in step with the Christian year.

New Daylight and the Bible

New Daylight contributors use a range of Bible versions, and you will find a list of the versions used opposite. You are welcome to use your own preferred version alongside the passage printed in the notes. This can be particularly helpful if the Bible text has been abridged.

New Daylight affirms that the whole of the Bible is God's revelation to us, and we should read, reflect on and learn from every part of both Old and New Testaments. Usually the printed comment presents a straightforward 'thought for the day', but sometimes it may also raise questions rather than simply providing answers, as we wrestle with some of the more difficult passages of scripture.

New Daylight is also available in a compact size edition. Visit your local Christian bookshop or BRF's online shop **brfonline.org.uk**. To obtain an audio version for the blind or partially sighted, contact Torch Trust for the Blind, Torch House, Torch Way, Northampton Road, Market Harborough LE16 9HL; +44 (0)1858 438260; **info@torchtrust.org**.

Comment on *New Daylight*

To send feedback, please email enquiries@brf.org.uk, phone **+44 (0)1865 319700** or write to the address shown opposite.

Writers in this issue

Inderjit Bhogal is a Methodist minister working with Churches Together in Britain and Ireland to develop and lead the Church of Sanctuary network.

Amanda Bloor is archdeacon of Cleveland, and has previously been a bishop's chaplain, a diocesan director of ordinands, an advisor in women's ministry and a parish priest.

Paul Gravelle was an Anglican priest in Auckland, New Zealand, as well as a poet, writer and retreat leader. He died in 2023.

Tim Heaton is rural dean of Blackmore Vale, an honorary canon of Salisbury Cathedral and the author of the best-selling Lent course *The Long Road To Heaven* (Circle Books, 2013). Connect with him at **facebook.com/lentcourses**.

Lakshmi Jeffreys inhabits assorted roles within and beyond the church, including wife, mother, sister, friend, dog-walker and priest.

Murdo Macdonald is policy officer with the Society, Religion and Technology project of the Church of Scotland, which looks at ethical issues in science.

David Runcorn is an Anglican priest, an author, a spiritual director and a retreat leader. His ministry has included local churches, Lee Abbey chaplain and a director of ordinands. You can meet him at **davidruncorn.com**.

David Walker is bishop of Manchester. He also chairs the board of USPG and is an active member of the UK House of Lords.

Jane Walters is chair of the Association of Christian Writers, an author, musician and former interior designer. **janewyattwalters.com**

Sally Welch is diocesan canon of Christ Church Cathedral, Oxford, and co-director of the Centre for Christian Pilgrimage. She is the former editor of *New Daylight*.

Catherine Williams is an Anglican priest working as a spiritual director and freelance writer. Catherine is also the lead voice on the Church of England's *Daily Prayer* and *Time to Pray* apps.

Veronica Zundel is an Oxford graduate, writer and columnist. She is the author of *Everything I Know about God, I've Learned from Being a Parent* (BRF Ministries, 2013).

Gordon Giles writes…

The Greek word, *ekklesia*, from which we get the word for 'church' in Latin, French and Welsh, comes from two Greek words – *ek* and *klesia*. *Ek* means 'out' and *klesia* means 'called'. The church are those who are called, not in but *out*. It is sometimes said, in the media if not elsewhere, that the church is going through a difficult time. Yet there have been difficult times before, none more so probably than in those early years of discipleship when many died for their faith, as many still do today.

Today's church is still made up of good, kind people, people who are sinners, we who hurt others, the damaged and the distressed, people of every gender, colour, race and denomination. We are the church. We are those who, as St Paul says, 'once were far off but have been brought near by the blood of Christ. For he is our peace; in his flesh he has made both into one and has broken down the dividing wall, that is, the hostility between us' (Ephesians 2:14, NRSV).

Paul is talking about Jews and Gentiles, but we have newer divisions and hostilities to contemplate and address. For it did not take long for the church to discover internecine strife, intellectual and spiritual argument, persecutions of its own and sectarianism. And now we are still coming up with new ones which jostle for attention.

Yet the church is not the arguments, the debates and the decisions. The church is the people of God, called in and out of our buildings to walk in the way of Christ, to live according to his teaching, to study his word and to love our neighbours as ourselves. No one, especially not Jesus, said it would be easy, nor that this calling would ever change.

Michael Ramsey, former Archbishop of Canterbury, wrote: 'The glory of Christianity is its claim that small things really matter and that the small company, the very few, the one man, the one woman, the one child are of infinite worth to God' (*The Christian Priest Today*, SPCK, 1972, p. 42). As we approach Christmas, devoting ourselves to meditating upon scripture, let us remember that we are all – each and every one of us – loved by God, who in Christ calls us to be the church on a shared journey of faith, hope and love.

GORDON GILES

The prayer of BRF Ministries

Faithful God,
thank you for growing BRF
from small beginnings
into the worldwide family of BRF Ministries.
We rejoice as young and old
discover you through your word
and grow daily in faith and love.
Keep us humble in your service,
ambitious for your glory
and open to new opportunities.
For your name's sake,
Amen.

'It is such a joy to be part of this amazing project'

As part of our Living Faith ministry, we're raising funds to give away copies of Bible reading notes and other resources to those who aren't able to access them any other way, working with food banks and chaplaincy services, in prisons, hospitals and care homes.

'This very generous gift will be hugely appreciated, and truly bless each recipient… Bless you for your kindness.'

'We would like to send our enormous thanks to all involved. Your generosity will have a significant impact and will help us to continue to provide support to local people in crisis, and for this we cannot thank you enough.'

If you've enjoyed and benefited from our resources, would you consider paying it forward to enable others to do so too?

Make a gift at **brf.org.uk/donate**

2 Thessalonians

Paul's second letter to the church of the Thessalonians is far from his most well-read epistle, yet it is probably one of his earliest. Some of the themes he develops here will go on to be expressed in more mature form, and in greater length and depth, in his letters to Rome and Corinth. Yet those are not good grounds for ignoring this part of his writings. As elsewhere, he is responding to the specific context of his readers which, as the founder of their church, he knows well. They are a minority faith, facing persecution and ridicule for their beliefs. And yet they have grown sufficiently, since Paul planted them, to be starting to experience divisions among their members. It is likely that they are in some form of contact with other Christian communities in other cities and regions. That will also be exposing them to a wider range of ideas and understandings of what exactly it is that God has been up to in Jesus.

In this early period, Christian theology is still in a developing phase. Many of the earliest believers had expected Jesus to come back in their own lifetimes and had planned for only a short span on earth. As those hopes dwindle, they need to begin to adjust to a long haul, and to face the kinds of issues that emerge as the original urgency abates. How is God going to bring all things to fulfilment, if he is not doing it imminently? What are the ground rules for sustaining a Christian community over a prolonged time? How can a community be inspired to go on striving to live and proclaim the gospel for a period that may last well beyond their lifetimes?

Paul addresses these questions, and he addresses them not as some remote theological sage, but as the one who founded their church, who has lived among them, and who takes proper pride in the way they have stuck to their task, growing in number and in faith notwithstanding the external and internal pressures they face. It is a warm letter, a deeply personal letter. One might almost call it a love letter.

DAVID WALKER

Expressing thanks

Grace to you and peace from God the Father and the Lord Jesus Christ. We must always give thanks to God for you, brothers and sisters, as is right, because your faith is growing abundantly and the love of everyone of you for one another is increasing. Therefore we ourselves boast of you among the churches of God for your steadfastness and faith during all your persecutions and the afflictions that you are enduring.

When I started chairing committees, I discovered that one of my duties was to thank those who were standing down at the end of their term of service. It is something I very much enjoy. The responsibility makes me reflect on the contributions each individual has made, alongside the personal attributes they have brought to our meetings, and then to put my gratitude and thanks into a few choice words. For a short while I am not concentrating on the challenges of the agenda, I am simply allowing my gratitude to flow. I invariably find that I am far more grateful than I have previously noticed.

In this early section of Paul's letter, he is doing the same. What he says is no mere flattery, designed to soften them up for the hard-hitting messages to follow. Paul offers genuine and deep gratitude for what one of the first Christian communities he had planted has achieved. Their circumstances have not been easy. They have faced persecutions and afflictions but have remained steadfast, growing in both faith and love. They provide an example that he can cite to the other, even newer, churches that he is founding.

Yet Paul is not just reminding them of their achievements, he is also offering up his thanks to God. Just as in human meetings we can focus too much on what we want done, so too our prayer life can be dominated by dwelling on what is wrong in the world or the church. Our devotions should not be dominated by lists of what we think God needs to put right.

Today's passage offers a challenge. Who do I want to thank God for?
And am I bold enough, like Paul was, to let them know
why I am so grateful?

DAVID WALKER

Hell and damnation

For it is indeed just of God to repay with affliction those who afflict you and to give relief to the afflicted as well as to us, when the Lord Jesus is revealed from heaven with his mighty angels in a fiery flame, inflicting vengeance on those who do not know God and on those who do not obey the gospel of our Lord Jesus. These will suffer the punishment of eternal destruction, separated from the presence of the Lord and from the glory of his might.

This passage does not read easily to a modern, western mind. That God afflicts wrongdoers, or that Jesus comes with angels, in flaming fire, to wreak vengeance against those who have persecuted his church, can come across as a relic of a bygone, more bloodthirsty age. The temptation is to quickly search for a more congenial paragraph, a few verses on. Yet Paul's words matter. They make clear that actions have consequences.

I have heard it said that while Christians may be required to believe in hell, they are not required to believe that anyone ends up there. I get that. I hope and pray that God's love and forgiveness will ultimately, even if beyond this human life, prove irresistible to every last soul. But God has blessed us with free will, including the choice to reject him utterly and finally.

One sign that a person may be on that path of rejection would be that they hate and persecute those who follow Jesus. It can be no easy matter, at the end of such a life, to accept God's welcome into his eternal and intimate presence. Paul knows from personal experience, having been himself a persecutor of the church, what a challenge it is to make a sudden and total about-face.

Yet beneath the harsh words of God's judgement in this passage I find a deeper mercy. The fate of any who have so deeply rejected God on earth that they cannot bear his presence in heaven is not the eternal torture so often depicted in medieval artwork, but simply to cease to be.

Who would I wish to see condemned to hell,
and how might I pray for them to accept God's love and mercy?

DAVID WALKER

Knocking on heaven's door

As to the coming of our Lord Jesus Christ and our being gathered together to him, we beg you, brothers and sisters, not to be quickly shaken in mind or alarmed, either by spirit or by word or by letter, as though from us, to the effect that the day of the Lord is already here. Let no one deceive you in any way, for that day will not come unless the rebellion comes first and the lawless one is revealed, the one destined for destruction.

Sometimes I wish we had access to the letters Paul received as well as those that he sent. It would be a blessing to know more about the situations he was trying to address instead of having to guess them from the answers he offers. Yet here, as in some other places, it seems that he is countering a view that the 'Day of the Lord' has already come.

Paul is writing only a couple of dozen years or so after the first Easter. Christians are still working out how their understanding of the way God will bring his creation to fulfilment relates to both the Jewish hope for a messianic era on earth and the Greek concept of the immortality of the soul. Eventually Christian theology will fuse around a resurrection that is both bodily (as was the resurrection of Jesus) but that primarily takes place beyond this life. Nevertheless, as John emphasises, for the Christian, judgement, and alongside it absolution, has already happened. The life we shall fully live in heaven is one we can begin to live here on earth.

However, Paul's young church are not there yet. Some are teaching them that the coming of Jesus has already brought the messianic age into being. Yet if that be the case, why are they still suffering? Why are their persecutors not being punished? Have they unknowingly failed God and are now experiencing his anger? 'Don't be fooled,' cries Paul. There is lots still to happen. Rebellion against God will get worse not better. This is how God's purposes must be worked out.

How do I live my life on earth so as to ready myself for the life of heaven?

DAVID WALKER

Lovers of truth

The coming of the lawless one is apparent in the working of Satan, who uses all power, signs, lying wonders, and every kind of wicked deception for those who are perishing because they refused to love the truth and so be saved... But we must always give thanks to God for you, brothers and sisters beloved by the Lord, because God chose you as the first fruits for salvation through sanctification by the Spirit and through belief in the truth. For this purpose he called you through our gospel, so that you may obtain the glory of our Lord Jesus Christ.

Back when my wife was teaching, a pupil, punished for some offence, would often react indignantly. They did so not because they had been falsely accused, but because they did not believe she had proof. By their logic, truth did not carry weight unless it could be proved conclusively.

Recent times have seen that principle carried into adult life, not least into the world of politics. Lies can be told, and told barefaced, as long as there is insufficient evidence to disprove them. Even when evidence someone has fought hard to conceal or destroy emerges to confound them, it can take a lot of public pressure for the culprit to apologise and resign.

Paul warns that lies and deception will be part of the troubles his young church will face. He could have been forgiven for advocating that they fight fire with fire, spreading their own untruths about their opponents. Indeed, Christians and their churches have sometimes done so. But for Paul, lies must be countered by the truth; we must be lovers of truth because God has chosen us to be bearers of the truth of Jesus.

Our witness to Jesus cannot be trusted if we show scant regard for truth elsewhere. It is a particularly stark warning to church figures who cover up wrongdoing to protect the reputation of a prominent leader or institution. Paul thanks his readers for their commitment to the truth, without which their proclamation of Jesus would be mere empty words.

When am I tempted to lie or distort the truth?
What step can I take today to be more truthful?

DAVID WALKER

Working for a living

Now we command you, brothers and sisters, in the name of our Lord Jesus Christ, to keep away from every brother and sister living irresponsibly and not according to the tradition that they received from us... For even when we were with you, we gave you this command: anyone unwilling to work should not eat. For we hear that some of you are living irresponsibly, mere busybodies, not doing any work. Now such persons we command and exhort in the Lord Jesus Christ to do their work quietly and to earn their own living.

Paul's early church communities may not have gone quite as far as the first Jerusalem Christians, who sold all their possessions and held the money raised in common. After all, it now looked less likely that Christ would return imminently; resources would need to be earned, not merely distributed. Nevertheless, they functioned as extended family units, meeting the needs of each from the wealth of all. It was a natural expression of Christian love and mutuality that members who were elderly, sick or young would be supported by those fit and able to work. Yet Paul is clearly responding to concerns that this mutuality is being exploited. There are those, well capable of work, who prefer to spend their time in idleness or unhelpful busybodying.

At times his words have been misconstrued – twisted to support arguments that the unemployed are lazy and feckless or to distinguish between the deserving and undeserving poor. Yet consistently my experience is that when such lines are drawn, they invariably maximise the proportion of the undeserving and minimise our shared responsibility for the alleviation of poverty. Myths are created of households who have happily lived off welfare payments for three generations or more. Or extremely rare examples, such as families deliberately choosing to have ten or more children, in order to live off the state, are splashed across the newspapers as though somehow typical.

Paul is not seeking to provide his readers with excuses to evade moral responsibility for their poorer, unemployed members. Rather he is urging everyone to find their productive place within the community, to make their contribution as part of the overall mission of Christ's church.

How am I playing my part as a labourer in Christ's service?

DAVID WALKER

When believers disagree

Take note of those who do not obey what we say in this letter; have nothing to do with them, so that they may be ashamed. Do not regard them as enemies, but admonish them as brothers and sisters. Now may the Lord of peace himself give you peace at all times in all ways. The Lord be with all of you. I, Paul, write this greeting with my own hand. This is the mark in every letter of mine; it is the way I write.

There is something remarkable in Paul's advice regarding those who fail to follow his instructions. Their false words are not to be listened to, but nevertheless they themselves are still to be treated as believers, not enemies. Continuing to hold them in the Christian family while not succumbing to their disobedience will, Paul assures his readers, ultimately make them ashamed.

History shows that so often Christians have done the opposite. Disagreement has led to schism, and schism has led to Christians declaring others to no longer be part of the faith. In my earlier days as a priest, I had some hope that this trajectory might be reversed. A lively ecumenical movement was slowly building reconciliation between denominations that had separated centuries before. Sadly, today I find groups even within one denomination, who hold to the same scriptures and creeds yet doubt each other's allegiance to Christ, doing exactly what Paul warned against.

Crucially, Paul does not end this theme with a warning but with words of blessing. He invokes God's peace and God's presence on all his readers, for that will be the strength in which they can fulfil his demands. Humanly, it is impossible, but with God the impossible happens.

Finally, and as he does in other letters, Paul signs his name with his own hand. It is a touching conclusion to a letter that had probably been largely written down by a scribe. Yet it is one through which he binds himself to the Thessalonian believers, and to all who will read and seek to follow his words both in his own era and for the generations to come, even to you and me.

How can I be a force for reconciliation,
both between individuals and in the church?

DAVID WALKER

Peter

'Too much is nearly enough.' That description might fit Simon Peter. Simon, the headstrong, impulsive, fisherman met Jesus and became Peter, a shepherd and a rock. (Peter was the only disciple in the gospels to be given a new name, although he is referred to as Simon when demonstrating to pre-Jesus behaviour.) Towards the end of his eventful life, he wrote to dispersed churches about how to manage persecution (1 Peter) and to a specific church to counteract false teaching (2 Peter). (Scholars debate the authorship of 2 Peter; here I assume that Peter was the author, if not the actual scribe.)

Peter is clearly a leader from the beginning and recognised as such by the writers of all four gospels, before accounts of his leadership of God's people in the book of Acts. Indeed, in each gospel, Peter is named first, whether among the twelve or when accompanied by James and John. He serves as an example of how ordinary people, not necessarily born to or bred for high office, who spend time with Jesus, can transform the world for God (Acts 4:13). Like many Christians, Peter had an initial call to follow Jesus, but there were other occasions when God 'called' him. We shall explore some of these in the studies.

Throughout the Bible, Peter's essential character remains the same. His passion, honesty, impetuosity, courage and tendency to go over the top become vehicles to reveal God's glory. Peter is a wonderful reminder that God takes us as we are and transforms us, without negating our history or our uniqueness. Everything we have experienced and everything we are can be offered in God's service. If you have time, skim read the gospels and Acts, focusing where you see Peter's name. Then read 1 and 2 Peter and discover how the rough-and-ready Galilean has become a wise mentor, able to share his story as required.

Finally, whether you identify with Peter's character or simply read with astonishment, I invite you to note Peter's responses to his circumstances and to Jesus. Above all, remember that God has chosen you as you are, with your history and personality, and by the Holy Spirit will remain with you and transform you. Peter was a special friend of Jesus. As you study, may your friendship with God deepen and grow.

LAKSHMI JEFFREYS

Chosen by God

Peter, an apostle of Jesus Christ, To the exiles of the dispersion in Pontus, Galatia, Cappadocia, Asia, and Bithynia, who have been chosen and destined by God the Father and sanctified by the Spirit to be obedient to Jesus Christ and to be sprinkled with his blood: May grace and peace be yours in abundance. Blessed be the God and Father of our Lord Jesus Christ! By his great mercy he has given us a new birth into a living hope through the resurrection of Jesus Christ from the dead.

Peter was called by Jesus on various occasions and in different ways. He knew what it was to be chosen from among others. How significant, therefore, for Gentile Christians undergoing persecution to be reminded that they too are special in God's sight. Despite their current hardship, they are acknowledged as God's people. However beleaguered, they are in receipt of God's unmerited favour (grace) and the deep recognition that all shall be well, regardless of circumstances (peace). And all this is offered by someone who knew what it was to suffer with and for Jesus. Peter speaks with authenticity about new birth and hope, because he has experienced life before, during and after Jesus' crucifixion and resurrection.

During the letter, Peter will outline to his hearers how to live in exile, how to endure threats to life and faith, and how to shine for Jesus. Perhaps this is one reason the message of Peter's first letter is timeless. Unlike sisters and brothers in Christ across the world (and in some communities in this country), I do not live in fear of my life.

Nevertheless, I am aware that my choices are not those advocated by social and other media. A Christian's purpose is not to amass wealth, seek power or pursue pleasure but to store treasure in heaven. Being chosen to love God and serve our neighbours automatically puts us at odds with those who have put themselves at the centre of their worlds.

Thank you, merciful God, that you have chosen us and you offer hope, despite what is happening to us or around us. Help us to take encouragement and learn from Peter's life and words. Amen.

LAKSHMI JEFFREYS

Call and response (1)

[Jesus] said to Simon, 'Put out into the deep water and let down your nets for a catch.' Simon answered, 'Master, we have worked all night long but have caught nothing. Yet if you say so, I will let down the nets.' When they had done this, they caught so many fish that their nets were beginning to burst… And they came and filled both boats, so that they began to sink. But when Simon Peter saw it, he fell down at Jesus' knees, saying, 'Go away from me, Lord, for I am a sinful man!'

I wonder why this experienced fisherman would take any notice when a lay person told him how to do his job. Perhaps Peter (still Simon at this point) was exhausted after a fruitless night's labour. Was his answer sarcastic? 'I'll let down the nets simply to prove how wrong you are, before I go home to bed.' On the other hand, in Luke 4:39 Jesus heals Peter's mother-in-law. If this happened before the miraculous catch of fish, it is less surprising that Peter should listen to the religious teacher.

Time and again, Peter recognises something special in Jesus and responds appropriately. His submissive words and actions remind me of Isaiah's woeful cry following a vision of God's holiness (Isaiah 6:5). As C.S. Lewis' Narnia stories emphasise, Aslan is not a tame lion. In other words, Jesus might be our friend and brother, but he is also the living God, who has power over all creation and ultimately over death itself.

Most of us do not experience huge miracles. It can be easy, especially in consumerist societies, to see Jesus as a divine slot-machine: we input prayers and God delivers the result we want. When prayers are apparently not answered, we might assume we have done something wrong or that God has not heard properly. When Peter's (unspoken) prayers are met beyond his imagination, he focuses not on the massive haul but on the one who brought it about and instinctively and dramatically worships.

Loving God, forgive me for the times I have attempted to 'tame' you.
Instead, please grant me the ability to see Jesus increasingly clearly,
that I might be awestruck again. Amen.

LAKSHMI JEFFREYS

Call and response (2)

When the disciples saw [Jesus] walking on the sea, they were terrified, saying, 'It is a ghost!' And they cried out in fear. But immediately Jesus spoke to them and said, 'Take heart, it is I; do not be afraid.' Peter answered him, 'Lord, if it is you, command me to come to you on the water.' He said, 'Come.' So Peter got out of the boat, started walking on the water, and came towards Jesus. But when he noticed the strong wind, he became frightened, and, beginning to sink, he cried out, 'Lord, save me!'

Whereas yesterday Jesus took the initiative, inviting Peter to try the other side of the boat for fish, today Peter speaks to Jesus. Of course, Jesus had already addressed the disciples to calm their fears. Was Peter checking that Jesus genuinely was not a ghost? Did he think this new method of crossing the lake was especially effective and worth attempting or simply incredibly 'cool'?

We shall not know this side of heaven. All we see is that Peter was fine until he took his eyes off Jesus and began to sink beneath the waves. Initially stunned by the miraculous catch of fish, the disciples now worship Jesus as God, after he and a soggy Peter return to the boat.

In this story, both Jesus and Peter show us who they are. Jesus is the Son of God, so the wind and waves obey his command. Meanwhile, Peter is a man of courage and faith. Yes, the faith is very small, but Jesus requires only a mustard seed's worth to relocate Tabor, Everest or any other mountain (Matthew 17:20)!

Faith is a gift of God, offering the ability to see and act on possibilities beyond the norm. The website **seenandunseen.com** offers Christian perspectives on almost anything – politics, leisure, even natural phenomena. When Peter looked at Jesus, he experienced the waves beyond anything he had known as a fisherman. Similarly, a friend of mine needs spectacles to perceive the physical world and uses the Bible to see beyond the physical and gain God's view.

Faithful Jesus, give me courage to respond to your call
and faith to see and experience the world as you do. Amen.

LAKSHMI JEFFREYS

17

A new name

Jesus replied, 'Blessed are you, Simon son of Jonah, for this was not revealed to you by flesh and blood, but by my Father in heaven. And I tell you that you are Peter, and on this rock I will build my church, and the gates of Hades will not overcome it. I will give you the keys of the kingdom of heaven; whatever you bind on earth will be bound in heaven, and whatever you loose on earth will be loosed in heaven.'

Lakshmi is the Hindu goddess of prosperity. My parents were convinced their first child would be a boy, so, when a daughter arrived instead, they decided they would need money – hence my name! In Jesus' time, as today, names signified purpose and character.

Immediately before the quoted text, Peter has acknowledged Jesus as the Messiah, the Son of the living God. Once again, he has perceived beyond the physical, seeing Jesus as God has revealed him (see yesterday's notes). In turn, Jesus expresses what he sees in Peter, beyond the immediate fisherman and Jonah's son.

Jesus' language here is prophetic – perhaps apocalyptic, as he reminds us that the spiritual world includes hell as well as heaven, evil in opposition to God's love and goodness. As such, we need to take care in making predictions about binding and loosing and Peter's status. Instead, recognise Jesus preparing Peter, whose name means 'rock', for the persecution he will undergo, some of which we see in the book of Acts and to which Peter refers in his letters. Indeed, if the kingdom of heaven is life under God's rule, then perhaps Peter 'unlocked' this at Pentecost. Whatever the ultimate significance, Peter's name from Jesus is a gift for a specific purpose.

You and I might not have a vocation involving a name-change. Nevertheless, we are called by God with a clear purpose – to love God with everything we are and to serve God and neighbour. The details will emerge on a daily basis, as they did for Peter in leadership of God's people. For now, we might need to recognise our general calling as God's beloved.

Be patient: Abram was 75 years old when God named him Abraham ('father of many' – Genesis 17:4–5). Isaac was born 25 years later!

LAKSHMI JEFFREYS

An old habit

From that time on, Jesus began to show his disciples that he must go to Jerusalem and undergo great suffering at the hands of the elders and chief priests and scribes and be killed and on the third day be raised. And Peter took him aside and began to rebuke him, saying, 'God forbid it, Lord! This must never happen to you.' But he turned and said to Peter, 'Get behind me, Satan! You are a stumbling block to me, for you are setting your mind not on divine things but on human things.'

Just when it appears Peter has got the hang of who and how Jesus is, he completely blows it! Immediately after supernatural revelation and prophetic utterance about Jesus' nature and purpose (see yesterday), the rock has become a stumbling block. It is not easy for Peter. He had been taught that the Messiah would ride into Jerusalem in glory. Suffering was definitely not part of the deal. How could this happen to the person Peter was beginning to see as the chosen one of God?

Peter's habit of saying what he sees and feels is not wrong, merely misinformed. Like most of us, Peter saw only what was before him, wearing spiritual blinkers. He forgot that we are in a spiritual battle and Satan comes disguised as an angel of light. He said what he thought was best for Jesus, rather than listening to Jesus and learning God's way. All of us assume we know what is right and can take matters into our own hands, occasionally with terrible consequences.

Today is the anniversary of the destruction of the Twin Towers in New York in 2001. Meanwhile, across the world people are killing civilians with the excuse that they are eliminating evil. When attempting to decide what is right or wrong, I need to focus on Jesus and remember that evil can only be fully defeated by God's love.

Loving God, as we remember that Jesus has gained the ultimate victory over Satan, give us the courage to look to you for the way to respond to atrocities in the world. Teach us to love people and hate evil and grant us the wisdom to recognise the difference. Amen.

LAKSHMI JEFFREYS

Whiter than white

Jesus took with him Peter and James and John and led them up a high mountain apart, by themselves. And he was transfigured before them, and his clothes became dazzling bright, such as no one on earth could brighten them. And there appeared to them Elijah with Moses, who were talking with Jesus. Then Peter said to Jesus… 'Let us set up three tents…' He did not know what to say, for they were terrified. Then a cloud overshadowed them, and from the cloud there came a voice, 'This is my Son, the Beloved; listen to him!'

During a talk last year, Bishop Ruth Bushyager asked how someone might describe colour to a person with colour blindness. She said Mark was doing something similar in trying to convey how Jesus appeared on the mountain. Peter, James and John were offered a vision of how Jesus would look in heaven. The bishop suggested it is appropriate to be terrified when you see and hear things so awe-inspiring and so far beyond anything you have ever before experienced that it defies description.

Equally appropriate is Peter's statement. While some commentators might accuse Peter of speaking before engaging his mind, I wonder if Peter has actually grasped the significance of Moses (through whom God delivered God's people and gave them the law) and Elijah (one who, during exile, foretold the future reign of God) alongside Jesus. Maybe Peter realised Jesus was the Messiah, who embodies the law and will deliver God's people once and for all. Perhaps Peter wanted to recall the Festival of Tabernacles: God's command for the people to stay in tents for a number of days and praise God for all God had given them in the land (Deuteronomy 16:13–17). Moreover, a voice from heaven possibly confirmed Peter's understanding, declaring who Jesus was and commanding the disciples to listen to him.

Throughout the Bible, people are given visions and experiences of the beauty or majesty of God. In every case, this is shortly before or after a major trial or period of suffering, probably to give reassurance of God's presence and power.

God of glory, thank you for revealing yourself to us
when we need you. Amen.

LAKSHMI JEFFREYS

Later reflections

So, dear brothers and sisters, work hard to prove that you really are among those God has called and chosen. Do these things, and you will never fall away... Therefore, I will always remind you about these things – even though you already know them and are standing firm in the truth you have been taught... For we were not making up clever stories when we told you about the powerful coming of our Lord Jesus Christ. We saw his majestic splendour with our own eyes... We ourselves heard that voice from heaven when we were with him on the holy mountain.

By the time Peter dictated this letter, he possibly knew he would not live much longer. Perhaps he took comfort in remembering how Jesus had told him he would lead God's people, then suffer and die. For Peter, being like Jesus was everything. This makes more poignant his passion for the ongoing discipleship of his hearers. God wants Christians to live in God's love – being patient, kind, forgiving, gentle, at peace with one another and in themselves. How hard this is! Yet Peter urges the believers to practise, to work hard, to live differently.

While others might claim the transfiguration (see yesterday) was a figment of the imagination, Peter is adamant that he and the others experienced all of this. As Tom Wright asserts in his commentary *Early Christian Letters for Everyone* (SPCK, 2014), Peter's personal account makes sense of all the Old Testament prophecies. He had heard God's voice saying, in effect, that Jesus was the promised Messiah. Now everyone was waiting until Christ returned in glory. The task until that day, was to pore over scripture to see how it matched what was said by those who personally met Jesus. Meanwhile, the small group of Christians could stand firm in the truth, especially as they recognised Jesus is the truth, as well as the way and the life.

Hope springs from living faithfully in Christ, and increasingly coming to know God through the Bible. The combination of personal testimony and diligent Bible study will enable church growth in numbers and discipleship.

Loving Father, thank you for people who share their stories of faith in Jesus.
Thank you, for people who help us understand the Bible.
Give us confidence to recognise the truth. Amen.

LAKSHMI JEFFREYS

I don't know him...

About an hour later someone else insisted, 'This must be one of them, because he is a Galilean, too.' But Peter said, 'Man, I don't know what you are talking about.' And immediately, while he was still speaking, the rooster crowed. At that moment the Lord turned and looked at Peter. Suddenly, the Lord's words flashed through Peter's mind: 'Before the rooster crows tomorrow morning, you will deny three times that you even know me.' And Peter left the courtyard, weeping bitterly.

A biopsy indicated she had cancer, but she was terrified of the disease and hospitals. In her desire to maintain an outward show of well-being, and perhaps because she wanted to be in control, she refused surgery and other treatment. Eventually, her body was riddled with malignant cells. In the final week of her life, with family and friends around her bed, she wailed her regret: why had she allowed fear to dominate her thoughts? Why had appearance been more important than dealing with reality?

Of course, Peter was terrified – crucifixion was barbaric. Peter loved his rabbi and had been adamant that he would never betray Jesus, regardless of what anyone else might do. This might have prompted Peter, after Jesus' arrest, to follow and hang around in the courtyard. Nevertheless, he could not bring himself to admit he was a disciple, despite the evidence for everyone to see and hear. Maybe, like the woman in the story, Peter's fear prevented him from facing the truth and acting accordingly. And then, as the cock crowed for the second time, Jesus' eyes met Peter's...

Peter's expression of his deep regret possibly saved his life. Judas Iscariot's realisation of his actions and their effects led to tragic consequences. Jesus' invitation to life in all its fullness (John 10:10) requires us to live with the world as it is, rather than as we would prefer.

Allow yourself sufficient time and perhaps, someone with whom you can share your thoughts and feelings as you say the prayer below.

God of power and hope, I hold before you [name what you fear or regret].
Please help me to live with this truth and make choices that will lead to
hope and peace, for me and for others involved. Amen.

LAKSHMI JEFFREYS

... but I want to know him.

Peter and the other disciple started out for the tomb. They were both running, but the other disciple outran Peter and reached the tomb first... Then Simon Peter arrived and went inside. He also noticed the linen wrappings lying there, while the cloth that had covered Jesus' head was folded up and lying apart from the other wrappings. Then the disciple who had reached the tomb first also went in, and he saw and believed – for until then they still hadn't understood the Scriptures that said Jesus must rise from the dead.

I wonder what observers thought about the race. John overtook Peter and arrived first, but Peter went into the tomb before his friend. They had to see for themselves whether what the women said was factual. It feels significant that in this account, Peter is also called Simon. Perhaps he was thinking and behaving as he used to, before he met Jesus. And yet, at the slightest possibility that Jesus' words were true, that he had been raised from the dead, Peter acted.

Although he did not yet know Jesus would completely forgive him, it seems that his bitter tears, as he realised his denial of Jesus and his inability to keep his promises (as we saw yesterday), allowed him to begin to make amends. Despite his feelings, Peter remained with the other disciples, so was able to hear the news for himself.

Sometimes we are the agents of things going dreadfully wrong, whether intentionally or otherwise. It is horrible to live with the consequences when our actions have adversely affected someone. While it might be tempting to hide away in shame, it is more important than ever to maintain contact with Christian friends, to carry on with daily life. For ages, I dreaded meetings where I might see a former colleague I had inadvertently hurt. At the same time, it was essential to rebuild that relationship. A wise spiritual director helped me to maintain perspective and inform my choices.

'Oh, what a miserable person I am! Who will free me from this life that is dominated by sin and death? Thank God! The answer is in Jesus Christ our Lord' (Romans 7:24–25, NLT).

LAKSHMI JEFFREYS

Restored

Jesus said, 'Feed my sheep… When you are old you will stretch out your hands, and someone else will dress you and lead you where you do not want to go.' Jesus said this to indicate the kind of death by which Peter would glorify God. Then he said to him, 'Follow me!' Peter turned and saw that the disciple whom Jesus loved was following them… When Peter saw him, he asked, 'Lord, what about him?'

I never fail to be moved by Jesus' encounter with Peter on the beach. Immediately before the quoted passage, Jesus addresses Simon (the name used when Peter is not engaging in God's way) and asks if he loves Jesus more than the others. What a perfect reminder of Peter's assertion that he would never fall away, whatever the others did! The third and final question uses a different word for love (*agape*), which implies deep friendship. Peter realises he has been restored three times and his betrayal has finally been forgiven. His status and vocation have been restored. At the same time, Peter is told he will be martyred because of Jesus. And just as at the very beginning, when he first called the fisherman, Jesus tells Peter to follow him.

How might you respond if Jesus told you the joys and sorrows to come in your life and then invited you to follow him? Peter's reaction is interesting: he turns away, notices John and moves the conversation from himself to someone else. Watch and listen to yourself and those around you when conversation becomes uncomfortably personal. Many of us try to change the subject completely or we talk about another person, whose circumstances might be similar. Jesus has no time for this and tells Peter to mind his own business!

Christian discipleship is expressed in community, but the responsibility for relationship with Jesus remains between Jesus and the individual disciple. The human condition leads us to compare ourselves to others, whether favourably or unfavourably. It takes constant practice to remember that someone else's story is theirs alone, unless they choose to share it on their terms. Perhaps a spiritual discipline is only ever to compare ourselves to Jesus!

Joy is a fruit of the Spirit; comparison is the thief of joy.

LAKSHMI JEFFREYS

3,000!

Amazed and astonished, they asked, 'Are not all these who are speaking Galileans? And how is it that we hear, each of us, in our own native language?'… But Peter, standing with the eleven, raised his voice and addressed them: 'Fellow Jews and all who live in Jerusalem, let this be known to you, and listen to what I say. Indeed, these are not drunk, as you suppose, for it is only nine o'clock in the morning. No, this is what was spoken through the prophet Joel.'

As they reflected on the events of Pentecost, perhaps the former fishermen should not have been surprised. After all, Jesus had informed them that they would fish for people. In addition, every time they fished as Jesus directed, the haul was immense!

Jesus has died, been raised from the dead and has returned to heaven. The disciples have been waiting together and suddenly, the Holy Spirit arrives. As an aside, one commentator noted that the ability to speak other languages was first given by God to the people at Babel, to make them unintelligible to one another and confuse them (see Genesis 11). Here the gift of other languages is given to address people in their own tongue – and there is still confusion! Peter, now the leader of the group, addresses the crowd. He ignores the slur implying that Galileans are less intelligent or educated than others, and speaks of God.

The gift of the Holy Spirit at Pentecost is sometimes referred to as the birthday of the church. Yet at this point the crowd is largely Jewish. They have gathered for the Festival of Weeks (related to the Festival of Tabernacles, mentioned in last Friday's reading). Peter offers the first sermon about how God has now fulfilled promises about the Messiah and has sent the Holy Spirit as a sign of the age to come. This would have made sense only to people who were familiar with the Old Testament.

Once again, Peter is following in Jesus' footsteps, bringing God's message of salvation and hope initially to his own people. We see the worldwide significance of this event. Peter was simply taking the next step with his Saviour.

Loving Jesus, may I walk faithfully with you
and trust you with the outcome. Amen.

LAKSHMI JEFFREYS

Healing

Peter looked intently at him, as did John, and said, 'Look at us.' And he fixed his attention on them, expecting to receive something from them. Peter said, 'I have no silver or gold, but what I have I give you; in the name of Jesus Christ of Nazareth, stand up and walk.' And he took him by the right hand and raised him up, and immediately his feet and ankles were made strong.

Jesus summoned Simon Peter to follow him (Luke 5:1–11) and later, in front of religious leaders and teachers in a crowded room, healed a paralysed man (Luke 5:17–26). Peter has been instrumental in 3,000 people choosing to follow Jesus. He then heals a paralysed man at the temple.

In both cases, the miracle is instant and the one healed and all onlookers give glory to God. The main difference is that Jesus first forgave the sins of the man lowered through the roof and thereby angered the Pharisees. Here, Peter heals the man in the name of Jesus Christ, to the chagrin of the religious leaders. (Read the rest of Acts 3 for the story.) As Peter, here with John, continues the work of Jesus to God's glory, he, like Jesus will encounter hostility from those in authority, as well as the wonder of the crowds.

As I reflect on this passage, I am struck by how Peter takes the miracle in his stride. Rather than giving money, which he did not have to spare, Peter gave the man the ability to walk, in the name of Jesus. It appears completely ordinary – God's kingdom is breaking in, so the lame will leap for joy (Isaiah 35:6).

In the 17th century, Brother Lawrence performed everyday tasks for God's glory in the power of the Holy Spirit. He became a monk, having been seriously injured as a soldier. His book *The Practice of the Presence of God* encourages Christians to follow Jesus not from their heads but their hearts. Perhaps, as we focus on Jesus in the everyday, we shall also transform lives.

'The Father loves the Son and shows him all that he himself is doing,
and he will show him greater works than these,
so that you will be astonished' (John 5:20).

LAKSHMI JEFFREYS

Peter and Cornelius

While Peter was still thinking about the vision, the Spirit said to him, 'Look, three men are searching for you… go with them without hesitation'… So Peter went down to the men and said… 'What is the reason for your coming?' They answered, 'Cornelius, a centurion, a righteous and God-fearing man who is well spoken of by the whole Jewish people, was directed by a holy angel to send for you to come to his house and to hear what you have to say.' So Peter invited them in and gave them lodging.

Cornelius has had a vision, telling him to meet Peter. Meanwhile, Peter, who has been praying and fasting, has a vision three times (again!) of God asking him to eat unclean food. Notice how Peter still feels that he knows best, contending that he has never eaten anything against the food laws, even after God's voice has challenged him to rethink (v. 14). A commentator mentioned the irony of Peter refusing food, while staying in the house of Simon the tanner, someone whose profession made him 'unclean'! Nevertheless, Peter invites the men to stay, then he accompanies them to meet Cornelius. Read the whole of Acts 10 to discover both the complexity and ease of Christian conversion.

Once again, Peter is acting true to type. He argues with God. He immediately goes to the door and then later goes to meet Cornelius. Now Peter is led by the Holy Spirit, rather than driven by desire. He is impulsive for Jesus, rather than reckless without an obvious purpose. His passion for holiness has grown, as he has experienced forgiveness and now fully lives in and for Christ. Sharing and living the gospel no longer depends on Peter but on the God who has called and sent him. If this means spending time with Gentiles, so be it.

If we are honest, all of us have ideas of how Christians should behave and, as a result, who really belongs to God. Many of these notions will come from our upbringing and traditions rather than God's Spirit. Perhaps it is important to fast and pray about our attitudes.

Pray for your own daily conversion to God's way of seeing and living.

LAKSHMI JEFFREYS

The rock, the cornerstone and living stones

Come to him, a living stone, though rejected by mortals yet chosen and precious in God's sight, and like living stones let yourselves be built into a spiritual house, to be a holy priesthood, to offer spiritual sacrifices acceptable to God through Jesus Christ.

Tom Wright's *Early Christian Letters for Everyone* (SPCK, 2014) explains the Old Testament background to this passage: God promised to send his Son and promised to build a house where he would live forever. Jesus Christ is the cornerstone of this building, the most precious of all. Hence, followers of Jesus, wherever they are and whatever their origin, abilities or current circumstances, are part of this new temple. Paul uses a similar metaphor about the church, the people of God, being where God's Holy Spirit lives and acts (1 Corinthians 3:16; Ephesians 2:22).

Peter knew the diversity of his hearers and the life-threatening challenges they faced. Here he gives them purpose and status in God's kingdom and will continue in the letter to outline what this means for their conduct. The main point remains that they, like Peter, have been chosen by God and will be transformed by the Holy Spirit.

God invites whom God invites. We do not choose our Christian brothers and sisters, but as we learn to see them as God does, together we grow into the most unlikely family. This is especially poignant for me as I write, as I am about leave our church and embark on the next step in my walk with Jesus. I have learned that people cannot read for a variety of reasons: because they are blind, or are under five years' and have not learned, or due to a disability from birth or a head injury. Similarly, some people in the congregation cannot walk: if they are babies or have had a stroke or are seriously ill or broke a leg. I long for people to meet our wildly diverse, wonderfully gifted church – yes, the people, not the beautiful, ancient building – and through them, see the amazing God who loves us into becoming his dwelling place.

---

*Praise God for the church across the world
and throughout history, built on Jesus Christ.*

LAKSHMI JEFFREYS

Zephaniah

 In many areas of life, there are things which we might consider insignificant and therefore unimportant. Languishing in the lower reaches of many sports, there are teams and individuals who battle on every week but will never get the attention that Manchester United or Andy Murray command. Were we to go on safari, we would look to spot the 'big five' animals (rhinoceros, leopard, lion, elephant and buffalo) – giving little thought to the many other organisms – including plants and bacteria – which are vital to the functioning of the ecosystem in which the bigger mammals survive.

In a similar way, towards the end of both the Old and New Testaments in our Bibles, there are collections of shorter books, most of which get largely ignored or skipped over. In the case of the Old Testament, these are often collectively referred to as 'the minor prophets', a term which alludes to the length of the book (as opposed to the much longer books of 'the major prophets', such as Isaiah or Jeremiah).

This terminology also unfortunately suggests that the minor prophets are of little significance – an idea which may be reinforced when you consider how infrequently you hear sermons preached from these texts. I confess to also being guilty as charged!

However, short as these books are – often extending to only a few hundred words – they nonetheless merit attention, bringing messages that remain relevant and impactful today. As we will see over the coming days, among the New Testament images and motifs which are found in the three short chapters of Zephaniah are: the impending judgement day of the Lord (Zephaniah 1; see also 2 Timothy 4:8); a sacrifice prepared by the Lord (Zephaniah 1:7–8; see also Revelation 19:17–18); and a mighty saviour (Zephaniah 3:17; see also Hebrews 12:2)

At first reading, the content of Zephaniah's prophecy is difficult and challenging. However, my prayer is that as you spend some time with this 'minor' prophet, you will find that he has some pretty 'major' things to say, and that you will be both challenged and encouraged in your faith.

MURDO MACDONALD

Who do you think you are?

The word of the Lord that came to Zephaniah son of Cushi, the son of Gedaliah, the son of Amariah, the son of Hezekiah, during the reign of Josiah son of Amon king of Judah. 'I will sweep away everything from the face of the earth,' declares the Lord.

In the TV programme *Who Do You Think You Are?*, celebrities are invited to trace their family roots, often making interesting and surprising discoveries on the way. It's popularity in the UK reflects a more general fascination with family trees, which has been sparked in part by the ability of the internet to make it easier for us to find out more about our (often long-lost) ancestry.

In Bible times, tracing your lineage was important – as shown in multiple genealogies recorded in scripture. Many of us who have set out to read our way through the New Testament have been daunted to be confronted with one such list of 'begats' in Matthew 1!

While we know little about the family backgrounds of many of the prophets, a potted genealogy of Zephaniah is set out at the beginning of the book that bears his name. And it is immediately clear that this is a family line to be proud of.

We are told that Zephaniah's great, great grandfather was named Hezekiah. Most likely this is highlighted to show that Zephaniah had royal blood. In the litany of royal reigns recorded in the book of 2 Kings, Hezekiah stands out as being one of the few kings who had a positive influence on the nation, leading them in the paths of God (see 2 Kings 18:5). Zephaniah 1:1 also tells us that he prophesied 'during the reign of [King] Josiah', another of the kings who led the nation in God's ways (see 2 Kings 23).

Godly leadership, whether in our nations, our churches or our families, is very important. We may take it for granted until it is no longer there. In the New Testament, Paul reminds us that to intercede for those in authority is of primary importance (1 Timothy 2:1–2), not, as is often the case, an afterthought once we have exhausted all other prayer topics.

Give thanks for people who have been godly influences in your life and in the lives of others.

MURDO MACDONALD

Setting the scene

'I will sweep away both man and beast; I will sweep away the birds in the sky and the fish in the sea – and the idols that cause the wicked to stumble. When I destroy all mankind on the face of the earth,' declares the Lord, '…. I will destroy every remnant of Baal worship in this place, the very names of the idolatrous priests – those who bow down on the roofs to worship the starry host, those who bow down and swear by the Lord and who also swear by Molek, those who turn back from following the Lord and neither seek the Lord nor enquire of him.'

Judgement is rarely a popular topic. As many sports fans know, there is endless scope for argument about refereeing decisions. Did the ball cross the line? Was that tackle fair? Should that be a penalty? Similarly, in family life, our siblings always seemed to be allowed to do things we never could.

One of the problems is that those making these judgements are fallible humans, with biases and incomplete views of the whole picture. While passages in the Bible where judgement is dispensed, such as today's one, may make us uncomfortable, we must remember that this is not true when God is the judge. Zephaniah reminds us that it is God who 'declares' (vv. 2–3).

In this opening salvo, a number of targets appear to be marked, including humanity and our fellow creatures. However, idolatry, the essential focus for God's judgement, is repeatedly identified: particularly those who claim to follow God (the priests in v. 4) while in fact bowing down to other deities. And as we are reminded in 1 Peter 2:9, all of us who are Christians are part of the 'royal priesthood'. We may not physically bow down to other gods, but most of us are aware that there are times when God does not reign supreme or alone, as he should.

Is there a thing beneath the sun,
That strives with Thee my heart to share?
Ah! tear it thence, and reign alone,
The Lord of every motion there.
Then shall my heart from earth be free,
When it has found repose in Thee.
(Gerhard Tersteegen, 1697–1769)

MURDO MACDONALD

The day of the Lord

Be silent before the Sovereign Lord, for the day of the Lord is near. The Lord has prepared a sacrifice; he has consecrated those he has invited… The great day of the Lord is near – near and coming quickly. The cry on the day of the Lord is bitter; the Mighty Warrior shouts his battle cry. That day will be a day of wrath – a day of distress and anguish, a day of trouble and ruin, a day of darkness and gloom, a day of clouds and blackness…. I will bring such distress on all people that they will grope about like those who are blind, because they have sinned against the Lord.

On 6 May 2023, the coronation of King Charles III, the UK monarch, took place in front of a large number of invited guests and was also witnessed by millions around the world. It was an occasion meticulously planned, with a great deal of pomp and ceremony. Many of those who played even a small part in the event will probably remember and reflect on that day for many years.

Some ideas and themes crop up repeatedly in scripture. The image of a 'day of the Lord' occurs on numerous occasions in the Bible, and in this section of the book (Zephaniah 1:7–18), the motif is very prominent. To introduce it, the prophet first calls for all to 'be silent before the Sovereign Lord' (v. 7), in awe of what is to come – a day that, we are told, God has prepared. Uncomfortable as we may find it, it becomes clear that this is an occasion of fearsome judgement: a day characterised by wrath, distress and ruin.

Two of the many other references to 'the day of the Lord' in other parts of the Bible are of particular interest. In his sermon on the day of Pentecost, Peter quotes from the prophet Joel (Acts 2:17–21). And in his second letter, Peter makes it clear that the 'day of the Lord' to end all days will come suddenly and with great destruction (2 Peter 3:10).

Have there been particularly momentous days in your life when you feel that God has spoken especially clearly to you?

MURDO MACDONALD

Bad neighbours

Seek the Lord, all you humble of the land, you who do what he commands. Seek righteousness, seek humility; perhaps you will be sheltered on the day of the Lord's anger... That land will belong to the remnant of the people of Judah; there they will find pasture. In the evening, they will lie down in the houses of Ashkelon. The Lord their God will care for them; he will restore their fortunes. 'I have heard the insults of Moab and the taunts of the Ammonites, who insulted my people and made threats against their land...', declares the Lord Almighty, the God of Israel... The Lord will be awesome to them when he destroys all the gods of the earth. Distant nations will bow down to him, all of them in their own lands.

The long-running Australian TV soap opera *Neighbours* centred on the lives of residents of Ramsay Street, a fictional neighbourhood. The opening line of the show's theme song reminds us of how important neighbours are – whether we have been involved in a dispute over maintenance of a shared fence or been grateful of a neighbour's willingness to take in a package which arrived when we were not at home.

At the national and international level, relationships with neighbours take on a whole new dimension. Trade across borders, access to shared resources, such as water, and quarrels about ethnicity, language, religion or tradition can be resolved amicably or can often lead to war.

Throughout the Bible, the nation of Israel was surrounded by larger, often hostile, states. This central section of Zephaniah (2:1—3:8) focuses on God's judgement of the regional neighbourhood – first of Judah (2:1–4), calling Jerusalem to repentance (3:1–8). The nation to the west of the God's people, the Philistines, is judged (2:4–7), then Moab and Ammon to the east (2:8–11). Finally, those to the south and north, Cush and Assyria (2:12–15), are called by God to account for their hostile actions and attitudes.

It helps, in the end, to have good neighbours.

Pray for those in your neighbourhood, asking that the light of God would shine brightly in their lives. Give thanks for good relationships and pray for any which require more work.

MURDO MACDONALD

Jerusalem, O Jerusalem

Woe to the city of oppressors, rebellious and defiled! She obeys no one, she accepts no correction. She does not trust in the Lord, she does not draw near to her God… Her prophets are unprincipled; they are treacherous people. Her priests profane the sanctuary and do violence to the law. The Lord within her is righteous; he does no wrong. Morning by morning he dispenses his justice, and every new day he does not fail, yet the unrighteous know no shame… 'Of Jerusalem I thought, "Surely you will fear me and accept correction!" Then her place of refuge would not be destroyed, nor all my punishments come upon her. But they were still eager to act corruptly in all they did.'

Being a parent is an enormous privilege, but it also comes with challenges. One issue is showing those in our care the right ways to behave. My now grown-up children often remind me that, when they were younger, if they forgot to say 'please' when asking for something, the request would be declined and they'd be told to wait five minutes then ask again.

God's fervent hope was that the people of Jerusalem, having seen the judgement on neighbouring nations, would turn back to him, seeking forgiveness. However, as laid out in graphic detail in this section, the sad truth becomes clear. Rather than accepting correction, the residents of the city, which has seen special blessing and protection over many years, continue their misbehaviour. The prophet describes them as being 'unprincipled' (v. 4), 'know[ing] no shame' (v. 5) and even 'eager to act corruptly' (v. 7). If we are honest, too often our own behaviour follows a similar (if perhaps not as extreme) pattern of going astray and refusing to accept correction.

From the beginning, Jesus' closest followers were called his 'disciples', which implies aspects of discipline. Paul reminded the Corinthian Christians of the need for self-discipline, comparing it to training for a race (1 Corinthians 9:25). As the writer to the Hebrews says, 'no discipline seems pleasant at the time, but painful. Later on, however, it produces a harvest of righteousness and peace for those who have been trained by it' (Hebrews 12:11).

'Discipleship is not that we work for God, but that God works through us'
(Oswald Chambers, 1874–1917).

MURDO MACDONALD

Restoration

'Then I will purify the lips of the peoples, that all of them may call on the name of the Lord and serve him shoulder to shoulder… On that day you, Jerusalem, will not be put to shame for all the wrongs you have done to me, because I will remove from you your arrogant boasters. Never again will you be haughty on my holy hill. But I will leave within you the meek and humble. The remnant of Israel will trust in the name of the Lord. They will do no wrong; they will tell no lies. A deceitful tongue will not be found in their mouths. They will eat and lie down and no one will make them afraid.'

When I was a student, one of the books which was almost mandatory reading for young Christians was John Stott's classic *Christian Counter-culture*. This in-depth study of Matthew 5—7 (the sermon on the mount) is still worth reading all these years later.

Near the beginning of the sermon on the mount are the beatitudes, which I suspect at least partly inspired Stott's title for his book. In these short statements, Jesus lays out an agenda which is contradictory to the standards of the world around us. Jesus asserts that blessedness (sometimes translated 'happiness') comes to those who are poor in spirit, merciful and pure in heart. These qualities are not the way to satisfaction that most of our contemporaries would espouse. Indeed, Jesus's original listeners probably felt as baffled as we are!

All the statements in the beatitudes are challenging and thought-provoking, but perhaps none more so than 'Blessed are the meek, for they will inherit the earth' (Matthew 5:5). Surely, if we do not speak up, we will be drowned out. In the real world, meekness is a way to be disinherited!

However, the themes and approaches Jesus talked about are exactly what we read here in Zephaniah. God makes it clear that he values meekness and humility (v. 12). In restoring his people, God will purify their lips (v. 9) and will remove those who boast and are haughty (v. 11). So we have here a foretaste of the counter-culture that Jesus came to bring.

Are there any books which have had an especially profound influence on your growth and development as a Christian? How and why?

MURDO MACDONALD

35

Sing out!

Sing, Daughter Zion; shout aloud, Israel! Be glad and rejoice with all your heart, Daughter Jerusalem! The Lord has taken away your punishment, he has turned back your enemy. The Lord, the King of Israel, is with you; never again will you fear any harm. On that day they will say to Jerusalem, 'Do not fear, Zion; do not let your hands hang limp. The Lord your God is with you, the Mighty Warrior who saves. He will take great delight in you; in his love he will no longer rebuke you, but will rejoice over you with singing… At that time I will gather you; at that time I will bring you home. I will give you honour and praise among all the peoples of the earth when I restore your fortunes before your very eyes,' says the Lord.

From lullabies to love songs, war chants to national anthems, much of human emotion finds expression in song. We come towards the end of this short prophecy, which has been uncomfortably dominated by themes of judgement, repentance and punishment. Near the beginning of this book, the people were told to be silent before God (Zephaniah 1:7). In these final verses, we find repeated reference to singing.

In verse 14, the people are encouraged to sing, to shout aloud and be glad with all their heart. This is not the embarrassed half-hearted mumbling we might be familiar with from school assemblies. This is full-throated belting it out – because there is a reason to do so! God, we are told 'has taken away your punishment… has turned back your enemy' (v. 15). After all the challenges they have faced, we are given a wonderful picture of God coming in redemption.

Perhaps even more striking is the image that we are given in verse 17. Not only is God the Mighty Warrior with his people in salvation, not only does his love mean he no longer rebukes them, even more amazingly, we have the picture of God himself 'rejoicing over [them] with singing', in much the way a doting grandparent might sing to a cherished infant. This is surely an image which makes us realise the extent of the love God has for his people.

Give thanks for those who are gifted in hymn- and song-writing
and who have helped enhance our worship through the centuries.

MURDO MACDONALD

Animals of the Bible

We share this wonderful planet with a dazzling array of other animals – fish, amphibians, reptiles, mammals, birds and insects – alongside which we have evolved over millions of years. The fossil record shows that multicellular animal life began on earth some 700 million years ago, emerging from the water on to dry land and then taking to the air. The dinosaurs, successors to one reptilian line, became extinct 65 million years ago after an asteroid impact. Their disappearance opened the door for the mammals that survived the collision to emerge from the dinosaurs' shadow and grow spectacularly in size and diversity. The evolutionary divergence of our human ancestors from the great apes began more than five million years ago, the species *Homo sapiens* being recognised from around 150,000 years ago.

This is a very different picture to that portrayed in the Bible. In a pre-scientific age, the creation stories of Genesis made helpful sense, but we must take notice of what God has more recently revealed to us through scientific discovery and reason. If we do this, we will be better able to appreciate our true place in God's created order, which is not set apart from the animal kingdom but part of it. We will become less anthropocentric in our outlook on the world and realise that our exploitation of the planet, which has devastating consequences for other animals, is simply not right. Who could say that God loves us more than sea turtles that have existed for more than 100 million years but are now critically endangered by our pollution of the oceans?

God's amazing creatures have a surprising number of walk-on parts in the Bible, though we hardly notice them because we are too busy thinking about what it all means for us. Not only do many pre-date us, but they will also be with us in the life of the world to come: the new creation is not promised to human beings alone; rather everything in God's good and present creation, all that God loves and treasures, will be transformed into something new and better and gathered into God's eternal future.

That is God's promise – to make *all things* new (Revelation 21:5), and for this 'the creation waits with eager longing' (Romans 8:19, NRSV).

TIM HEATON

Camel

Jesus said to his disciples, 'Truly I tell you, it will be hard for a rich person to enter the kingdom of heaven. Again I tell you, it is easier for a camel to go through the eye of a needle than for someone who is rich to enter the kingdom of God.' When the disciples heard this, they were greatly astounded and said, 'Then who can be saved?' But Jesus looked at them and said, 'For mortals it is impossible, but for God all things are possible.'

One wonders why Jesus chose a camel to illustrate his point. Some say it is a typo, the Greek word for 'rope' being just one letter different from the word for camel. (Rope would be more consonant with needle while still preserving the sense of impossibility.) The story of a tiny gate in the Jerusalem wall called the Needle's Eye, too small for a loaded camel to pass through, is untrue. Most probably the maxim of camel and needle was a traditional saying, but the important thing is this: it is not merely hard for a rich person to enter the kingdom of God, it is impossible.

Camels are first mentioned in the Bible in the days of the Patriarchs, though the Hebrew and Greek words, like our own word 'camel', do not distinguish between the one-humped dromedary of Arabia (*Camelus dromedarius*) and the two-humped Bactrian camel of Central Asia (*Camelus bactrianus*). Both have the capacity for storing fat in their humps and converting it to water.

Despite John the Baptist wearing clothing of camel's hair (Matthew 3:4), camels were not common in Galilee and Judea, being used only by desert peoples who valued them for their ability to travel long distances without water.

The beauty of this story is in its ending: while it remains impossible for a rich person to enter the kingdom of heaven, for God all things are possible (v. 26). Humanly speaking the situation in question is not possible, but God's power is not limited by such constraints. God can save anyone, even the rich, and that is the triumph of grace.

God of grace, we rejoice in our salvation, which is not any kind of achievement of our own but your work in Christ alone. Amen.

TIM HEATON

Dog

Now the woman was a gentile, of Syrophoenician origin. She begged [Jesus] to cast the demon out of her daughter. He said to her, 'Let the children be fed first, for it is not fair to take the children's food and throw it to the dogs.' But she answered him, 'Sir, even the dogs under the table eat the children's crumbs.' Then he said to her, 'For saying that, you may go – the demon has left your daughter.' And when she went home, she found the child lying on the bed and the demon gone.

Did this woman catch Jesus in a bad mood with his compassion down? The harshness of his analogy, which compares Gentiles to dogs, seems to border on hostility, leading some interpreters to want to lessen the shock by suggesting Jesus was referring affectionately to puppies or pet companions. Not so. While the word translated 'dogs' does suggest household animals rather than feral or stray dogs, there is no getting away from the fact that this is an insulting metaphor, although this was a style of oral combat quite common in its time.

It is generally agreed that the dog (*Canis familiaris*), a descendant of the wolf, was the first animal ever to be domesticated, and by the late Stone Age was kept in many parts of the world, often for hunting. In Jewish culture, dogs were not typically kept as household pets; rather they were semi-wild animals that roamed outside the city walls scavenging for rubbish, were potential carriers of disease and by their very nature unclean.

Jesus initially rebuffs the woman's plea for help, suggesting that his ministry is to Israel ('the children') first, but he ends up conceding the verbal sparring match. Her response turns the demeaning metaphor to her advantage, and when Jesus recognises that her argument is stronger than his he grants her request – a very human moment.

In the end, the miracle is about not only healing but also the overcoming of prejudice and boundaries, an event that points to a future in which Gentiles will be included in God's plan for the world and where their faith will bring salvation.

God of all people, may we learn from your Son how to lose an argument and how to show the same graciousness. Amen.

TIM HEATON

Donkey

The next day the great crowd that had come to the festival heard that Jesus was coming to Jerusalem. So they took branches of palm trees and went out to meet him, shouting, 'Hosanna! Blessed is the one who comes in the name of the Lord – the King of Israel!' Jesus found a young donkey and sat on it, as it is written: 'Do not be afraid, daughter of Zion. Look, your king is coming, sitting on a donkey's colt!'

In 1917, the penultimate year of World War I, Jerusalem fell into the hands of the British Army. As General Sir Edmund Allenby rode down the Jaffa Road, poised to enter the holy city by the Jaffa Gate, any Christ-like pretensions were avoided as the Foreign Office sent a telegram: 'Strongly suggest dismounting!' It would be far better if the general entered the city on foot. The way you do these things is important; you want to give out the right signals.

All four gospels narrate the story of Jesus' triumphal entry into Jerusalem, and all have him riding either a donkey or a colt, the foal of a donkey. The donkey (*Equus asinus*) is a domesticated ass, descended from the wild ass, and known to have been used as a beast of burden since 4000BC. Donkeys are first mentioned in the Bible as being owned by Abram in Egypt (Genesis 12:16), who had presumably used them as transport for his family and possessions on the journey from Haran.

From very early times it had become regarded as improper for monarchs to ride a horse in peacetime. Horses were associated with war, and so on other occasions royalty would ride donkeys to demonstrate their peaceful intentions. This is the context for Jesus' entry into Jerusalem and the evangelist's quote from Zechariah 9:9 (v. 15), making the twofold point that Jesus *is* a king (albeit not of this world), but not the warring ruler who would gain his objectives by force. The humble donkey makes Jesus' purpose clear: no warhorse for this meek and gentle king, who comes in peace.

King of kings, prince of peace, your kingdom is a peaceable kingdom.
And so we pray: your kingdom come, your will be done. Amen.

TIM HEATON

Dove

Then [Noah] sent out the dove from him to see if the waters had subsided from the face of the ground, but the dove found no place to set its foot, and it returned to him to the ark, for the waters were still on the face of the whole earth… He waited another seven days, and again he sent out the dove from the ark, and the dove came back to him in the evening, and there in its beak was a freshly plucked olive leaf; so Noah knew that the waters had subsided from the earth.

By the time this narrative was written, the olive tree was already a familiar symbol of peace and flourishing life, emanating from ancient Greece. The consequence of the story, in which the flood waters have subsided enough to show that God has made peace with the earth – metaphorically 'extending an olive branch' – is that the dove itself becomes a symbol of peace. In situations of conflict resolution, those who seek conciliation are called 'doves', while those who advocate more aggressive policies are 'hawks'.

Several species of dove (*Columbidae*) are found across the world, closely related to the ubiquitous wood pigeon (*Columba palumbus*). There are rock doves and stock doves, collared doves and turtledoves, the latter being named in the Bible as the required sacrifice for purification after childbirth (Leviticus 12:8; Luke 2:24). St Columba, the great missionary of Iona, took his name from the dove and was otherwise known as Colum Cille, 'dove of the church'.

At the baptism of Jesus, all four gospels record that the Holy Spirit descended on him 'like a dove'. The Spirit was not a dove but appeared as something *like* a dove. The origin of the simile has never been neatly reduced to a single explanation, but inevitably one thinks of Noah and his dove of peace, and also of the Spirit of God that hovered – perhaps fluttering like a bird – over the chaotic waters before the creation (Genesis 1:2, NIV). One way or another, the dove has forever secured its place in Christian art as a symbol of both peace and the Holy Spirit.

Reconciling God, may we submit ourselves to your Spirit
and know the real peace that comes from your presence. Amen.

TIM HEATON

Fish

[Jesus] got into one of the boats, the one belonging to Simon, and asked him to put out a little way from the shore. Then he sat down and taught the crowds from the boat. When he had finished speaking, he said to Simon, 'Put out into the deep water and let down your nets for a catch.' Simon answered, 'Master, we have worked all night long but have caught nothing. Yet if you say so, I will let down the nets.' When they had done this, they caught so many fish that their nets were beginning to burst.

The Sea of Galilee is an inland freshwater lake, about 13 miles long and eight miles wide, fed from the north by the river Jordan. Here, probably at Capernaum, Jesus called his first disciples, Simon, Andrew, James and John, who were partners in the same fishing enterprise (Luke 5:10). Luke's account of the miraculous catch of fish, which comes *before* the four fishermen are called, provides a plausible reason why they 'left everything and followed him' (v. 11). John places a similar story at the end of the fourth gospel.

Fish was a staple food in first-century Palestine and a thriving fishing industry flourished on the lake, as it does to this day. More than 20 species of fish can be found in the lake, often in large shoals, including tilapia or 'St Peter's fish' (*Chromis simonis*), a rather bony fish routinely eaten by pilgrims to the Holy Land, in my case without much delight. This is said to be the fish that produced a coin from its mouth for payment of the temple tax (Matthew 17:27).

The fishermen are called as disciples to participate in God's mission to the world, and fishing becomes a metaphor for gathering men and women into the kingdom. This is our calling, too. Our missionary work will meet with failures and frustrations and there will be times when we catch nothing. But do not despair: our task is simply to cast the net. On that alone will we be judged, not on the catch, which the Lord himself will provide.

Missionary God, you are full of surprises. At your command
may we put out into the deep water and let down our nets. Amen.

TIM HEATON

Fox

Now when Jesus saw great crowds around him, he gave orders to go over to the other side. A scribe then approached and said, 'Teacher, I will follow you wherever you go.' And Jesus said to him, 'Foxes have holes, and birds of the air have nests, but the Son of Man has nowhere to lay his head.' Another of his disciples said to him, 'Lord, first let me go and bury my father.' But Jesus said to him, 'Follow me, and let the dead bury their own dead.'

These would-be followers of Jesus have their understanding of discipleship seriously challenged: the follower must be like the one who is followed. To be called to follow Jesus is to be summoned to a life in which all the world's priorities of comfort and security are tested. The irony is that while creatures of the field and sky have somewhere to live, the Son of Man, who is Lord of all creation, is a wanderer with no place to call home.

The species of fox that we know best is the red fox (*Vulpes vulpes*), present across the entire northern hemisphere. Foxes are social animals that live in loose family groups in underground dens – Jesus paints a homely picture. Yet life is not easy for foxes – as destructive predators, valued for their fur and chiefly responsible for the spread of rabies, they are much hunted. But the fox is a born survivor, crafty and cunning.

On another occasion, Jesus refers to Herod as 'that fox' (Luke 13:32), a passage we shall look at tomorrow when we turn to the hen – a popular dinner for foxes.

There is a place provided by nature for animals, but the Son of Man has nowhere to live. The clear implication is that if Jesus has no place to call home, then neither will those who seek to follow him. This sounds harsh on our ears today, but it stands as an indication of the radical demands of discipleship: the call to follow Jesus must be set above every other care, whether for self or family – even for the dead (v. 22).

God of all life and love, you have a home in my heart:
perhaps together we can do something good today. Amen.

TIM HEATON

Hen

At that very hour some Pharisees came and said to [Jesus], 'Get away from here, for Herod wants to kill you.' He said to them, 'Go and tell that fox for me, "Listen, I am casting out demons and performing cures today and tomorrow, and on the third day I finish my work. Yet today, tomorrow, and the next day I must be on my way, because it is impossible for a prophet to be killed outside of Jerusalem." Jerusalem, Jerusalem, the city that kills the prophets and stones those who are sent to it! How often have I desired to gather your children together as a hen gathers her brood under her wings, and you were not willing!'

Herod, Tetrarch of Galilee, is a fox – sly and predatory. Although he wants to kill Jesus, just as he commanded the death of John the Baptist, he will not: Jesus will end his divinely appointed mission in Jerusalem. He *must* be on his way (v. 33). He does not go to Jerusalem to escape death but to die there. He shall be killed there just as the prophets were killed there.

Foxes are notorious for raiding farmyards for chickens, so it seems natural that the image of a fox (Herod) in Jesus' mind should move directly to that of a hen protecting her chicks. A hen is the female bird of the domestic fowl (*Gallus gallus*). It is not mentioned once in the Old Testament, and only here (and in the parallel passage in Matthew) in the New Testament. For this we must be thankful, for what more tender image could be given?

Jesus' lament over Jerusalem is cherished for this beautiful simile of God's love, which is like a mother hen that draws her young under her wings when danger threatens. Maternal images of God are rare in the Bible, but this is one of them and it is rightly treasured. But what sadness: the children of Jerusalem are exposed but they will not accept God's protection. Instead, Jerusalem will betray God by rejecting his son. Fateful events lie ahead and these verses loom as portents.

Mothering God, rejected by many, may I find shelter and safety under your wings and rejoice in your protection. Amen.

TIM HEATON

Horse

'Do you give the horse its might? Do you clothe its neck with mane? Do you make it leap like the locust? Its majestic snorting is terrible. It paws violently, exults mightily; it goes out to meet the weapons. It laughs at fear and is not dismayed; it does not turn back from the sword. Upon it rattle the quiver, the flashing spear, and the javelin. With fierceness and rage it swallows the ground; it cannot stand still at the sound of the trumpet.'

Job's response to adversity takes up the question of undeserved suffering – the affliction of the innocent. Job complains to God, is rebuked by his friends and then answered by God. In Job 38—39, God essentially asks: 'What do you know? Can you do what I do?' And against the inventory of cosmic wonder and natural beauty that follows, Job abandons his challenge of God's ways.

It is one of my favourite parts of the Bible, definitely worth a read if you can find a few minutes to do so. A dozen animals are mentioned in a spectacular tour of creation, from which I have selected the horse (*Equus caballus*) for no reason other than to draw attention to its association throughout the Bible with war and power, as we touched upon on Tuesday when we considered the donkey. Before 'man's inhumanity to man' took hold upon the earth, the ancestors of the horse roamed wild and free in the grasslands of Europe and Asia, beautiful and graceful animals whose exploitation as instruments of war is a stain upon humanity.

There are horses in heaven. Revelation 6 tells of four riders mounted on horses of different colours – the four horsemen of the apocalypse, emissaries of God sent to inflict divine punishment on the world for its sin. But there is another horse, whose rider is 'the Word of God' (Revelation 19:13), who leads the armies of heaven. This horse is a warhorse, too, but the war is a war on injustice, inequality and want. Its rider is the Messiah, and his white horse symbolises victory.

God of righteousness, your word is a sharp sword in my hand.
May I wield it only for good in the fight against evil. Amen.

TIM HEATON

Lion

Then Samson went down with his father and mother to Timnah. When he came to the vineyards of Timnah, suddenly a young lion roared at him. The spirit of the Lord rushed on him, and he tore the lion apart bare-handed as one might tear apart a kid... Then he went down and talked with the woman, and she pleased Samson. After a while he returned to marry her, and he turned aside to see the carcass of the lion, and there was a swarm of bees in the body of the lion and honey. He scraped it out into his hands and went on, eating as he went.

'Out of the eater came something to eat. Out of the strong came something sweet' (Judges 14:14). This is the riddle that Samson subsequently put to his wedding guests, following his discovery of the honey, a story immortalised since 1883 – somewhat oddly – in the green-and-gold logo of Lyle's Golden Syrup! The lion appears many times in scripture as a symbol of courage and strength, here giving us an indication of Samson's legendary and abnormal physical strength.

Lions were once found throughout the Middle East but have now disappeared from Bible lands. The last lion in Palestine is thought to have been killed in the 13th century. This Asiatic lion (*Panthera leo persica*), which closely resembles the African lion (*Panthera leo leo*), is now only found in very small numbers in the Indian state of Gujarat. Because of human-induced threats – climate change, habitat loss and poaching – most populations of African lions are in decline today, the shameful result of human selfishness and greed.

'Lion of Judah' is one of the messianic titles of Christ found in Revelation 5:5 (an allusion to Genesis 49:9), portraying Jesus as the culmination of the courage and strength of the tribe of Judah, the conquering lion worthy to open the seven seals of judgement. Throughout history the lion has also been an emblem of royalty and power, a winged lion becoming the symbol of St Mark the Evangelist in recognition of his gospel that points to the majesty of Christ.

Lord of all creation, stir the hearts of your people to love every creature that you have made as much as you love them. Amen.

TIM HEATON

Pig

Then Jesus asked him, 'What is your name?' He replied, 'My name is Legion; for we are many.' He begged him earnestly not to send them out of the region. Now there on the hillside a great herd of swine was feeding, and the unclean spirits begged him, 'Send us into the swine; let us enter them.' So he gave them permission. And the unclean spirits came out and entered the swine, and the herd, numbering about two thousand, stampeded down the steep bank into the sea and were drowned in the sea.

The Gerasene demoniac lives among the tombs of the dead, shackled and howling like a wild animal. Even chains cannot subdue him; he wrenches them apart and injures himself repeatedly on the rocks. The demons have stripped him of every shred of humanity. The demons' name, Legion, suggests a very large number: a Roman legion comprised 6,000 infantry, though the word could also refer to a battalion numbering about 2,000 men, which matches the number of pigs in the herd.

All breeds of pig (*Sus domesticus*) are descended from the wild boar. The Israelites were divinely prohibited from eating pig, notionally because 'it does not chew the cud' (Leviticus 11:7), but for more practical reasons because it is a scavenger and hosts the parasite that can cause trichinosis in humans if the meat is insufficiently cooked. Its classification as an unclean food led to the pig becoming more generally despised and hated.

Legion strikes a bargain with Jesus: instead of expelling the demons from the territory might he permit them to enter the pigs? Jesus obliges, but there is a twist in the tale and they end up drowned in the sea. It is natural for us to question the ethics of this, feeling sorry for the pigs and lamenting the economic loss incurred by their owner. But to a Jewish audience, the destruction of the abhorrent herd along with the demons would have been regarded as a doubly good conclusion to the story – a story that is not really about pigs at all but the transforming power of God.

Loving God, your healing power can overcome the worst evils in human experience: we pray for all who need that transformation today. Amen.

TIM HEATON

Scorpion

'So I say to you, Ask, and it will be given to you; search, and you will find; knock, and the door will be opened for you. For everyone who asks receives, and everyone who searches finds, and for everyone who knocks, the door will be opened. Is there anyone among you who, if your child asked for a fish, would give a snake instead of a fish? Or if the child asked for an egg, would give a scorpion? If you, then, who are evil, know how to give good gifts to your children, how much more will the heavenly Father give the Holy Spirit to those who ask him!'

What sort of parent would give their child a scorpion instead of an egg? Such a cruel substitution must surely make Jesus' question a hypothetical one, drawing the conclusion that if a human parent will give their children only good things, then how much more will our Father of greater goodness give us? He will give the Holy Spirit – the greatest gift – to those who ask.

The scorpion (*Scorpiones*) is a largely nocturnal creature that lives mainly in deserts, spending the day hidden under stones or in holes and emerging at night to hunt the small animals on which they feed. They have large fore-pincers and a long up-turned tail ending in a stinger. One of the first animals to live on land full-time, their evolutionary history goes back over 400 million years.

In his series of paintings 'Christ in the Wilderness', Stanley Spencer included one entitled *The Scorpion*. It shows Jesus sitting on the ground, contemplating a scorpion in his open hands. The hand that holds the scorpion is slightly swollen, suggesting that the scorpion has already stung him. What is the meaning? Has God the Father given his own Son a scorpion instead of an egg? Perhaps the answer is yes – he has given him the sting of death. Jesus must die in order to overcome death, and through the cross he takes the sting of death from us: 'Where, O death, is your victory? Where, O death, is your sting?' (1 Corinthians 15:55).

Father of all goodness, God who gives, thank you for your Son Jesus,
who you gave that I may have eternal life. Amen.

TIM HEATON

Sheep

'I am the good shepherd. The good shepherd lays down his life for the sheep. The hired hand, who is not the shepherd and does not own the sheep, sees the wolf coming and leaves the sheep and runs away, and the wolf snatches them and scatters them. The hired hand runs away because a hired hand does not care for the sheep. I am the good shepherd. I know my own, and my own know me, just as the Father knows me, and I know the Father. And I lay down my life for the sheep.'

Throughout the Bible, shepherds and sheep have deep metaphorical significance. To be a shepherd was an honourable calling – Moses and David were among them – and a portrayal in Ezekiel 34 of God as the true shepherd of Israel is carried over in John's gospel to Jesus as the good shepherd.

Shepherds lead, protect, feed and rescue their sheep, caring for the weak, the injured and the lost. In turn, the sheep becomes an image of humankind: helpless, easily led astray, unable to fend for itself or find its way home. In the New Testament, the only entirely non-figurative references to sheep are that they were sold in the temple for sacrifices.

The sheep (*Ovis aries*) was first kept by Neolithic man 7,000 years ago. Its ancestors were mountain sheep domesticated for their milk, meat and wool, the milk being used in the form of curds as a basic foodstuff and more important than the meat because of its sustainability. The wool became very valuable, being the most easily available fibre for clothing.

The pastoral (literally 'of land used for grazing') image of Jesus as a shepherd has led to the church's characterisation of its leaders as 'pastors' involved in 'pastoral care', but John 10 pushes further in its reference to the shepherd's willingness to lay down his life for the sheep. (Note that he lays down his life for *the* sheep, not *his* sheep, which makes it an inclusive rather than an exclusive gift.) It unfolds for us the great paradox of the gospel: the shepherd himself becomes the sacrifice.

True and good shepherd of the flock, I will follow you today
wherever you lead me, trusting in your care and provision. Amen.

TIM HEATON

Snake

'Very truly, I tell you, we speak of what we know and testify to what we have seen, yet you do not receive our testimony. If I have told you about earthly things and you do not believe, how can you believe if I tell you about heavenly things? No one has ascended into heaven except the one who descended from heaven, the Son of Man. And just as Moses lifted up the serpent in the wilderness, so must the Son of Man be lifted up, that whoever believes in him may have eternal life.'

To showcase the snake, you might have expected to read the story of the serpent in the garden of Eden. But, as I wrote in the Introduction, I think it best if we move on from the garden and try to understand how the real biological world evolved and see the richness of God's creation as it truly is. So instead, we have a saying of Jesus that alludes to an episode during the Israelites' wilderness years: with the people plagued by snakebites, Moses is instructed by God to make a serpent of bronze and set it on a pole, so that 'everyone who is bitten shall look at it and live' (Numbers 21:8).

The snake (*Serpentes*) is a sub-order of reptiles found in all habitats of the world, from desert to woodland to marsh. There are around 600 venomous species, of which about 200 can kill a human, so it is hardly surprising that snakes are widely regarded with terror and are the object of phobias and that throughout the Bible snakes appear as an image of the power of evil.

A snake on a pole is a symbol widely used around the world today by paramedics and other emergency medical services, but in John's gospel healing is not the only thing in view. The key to interpreting the analogy with the Son of Man is in the Greek 'lifted up' (v. 14), meaning both physically lifted up (on the cross) and 'exalted'. John employs the double meaning intentionally: it is only in his crucifixion that Jesus is exalted by God.

Suffering God, thank you for the glory of the cross, an instrument of humiliation that became the means of exaltation. Amen.

TIM HEATON

Whale

Nevertheless, the men rowed hard to bring the ship back to land, but they could not, for the sea grew more and more stormy against them. Then they cried out to the Lord, 'Please, O Lord, we pray, do not let us perish on account of this man's life. Do not make us guilty of innocent blood, for you, O Lord, have done as it pleased you.' So they picked Jonah up and threw him into the sea, and the sea ceased from its raging… But the Lord provided a large fish to swallow up Jonah, and Jonah was in the belly of the fish three days and three nights.

Everybody knows that Jonah spent three days in the belly of a whale – only it was not a whale, it was a 'large fish' (v. 17). Yet despite the Hebrew nomenclature, the creature that swallowed Jonah could have been a sperm whale (*Physeter macrocephalus*), which have been observed in the eastern Mediterranean Sea.

Whales are not fish; they are mammals – they are warm blooded (fish are cold blooded); they breathe air through lungs (fish use gills to extract air from water); and they give birth to live young (most fish, with some exceptions, lay eggs). The blue whale (*Balaenoptera musculus*) is the largest living animal of our time, up to 30 metres in length and weighing nearly 200 tons.

In the gospels, Jesus speaks of the 'sign of Jonah'. In Matthew, the sign points to the time when the Son of Man will spend three days in the darkness of the tomb (Matthew 12:40). But in Luke, the sign is Jonah himself and his call to repentance. The people of Nineveh repented as a result of Jonah's message, but the people of Jesus' own time have not been receptive to Jesus and his proclamation of the kingdom. They have heard someone far greater than Jonah but have not listened. They ask for a sign but none will be given other than the sign of Jonah: hear the word of God and do his will, just as the Ninevites did (Luke 11:29–32).

God of Jonah, your Son is greater than any prophet; may his word inform all that I think and say and do, today and always. Amen.

TIM HEATON

Colossians

 Paul wrote this letter to the church in the small town of Colossae around AD62. Along with Ephesians, Philippians and Philemon, it was written while he was in prison, likely in Rome. Although the church had been established during his third missionary journey, Paul himself was not the founder. Instead, that honour fell to Epaphras, a convert from the area, whom Paul commends warmly in this message.

As ever, Paul manages to deliver strong doctrinal teaching with a pastoral edge. These believers were important to him. Where he brings correction, it is for their good and indeed ours. For context, it seems that visitors had arrived at the church bringing teaching that was not entirely true to the gospel. This is the danger of all errant teaching: that it has enough truth in it to make it both plausible and palatable. With its shift in emphasis here, an addition and subtraction there, the young church was in danger of being blown off-course. It is a danger we cannot ignore today.

Chief among their claims was that there was more to salvation than Jesus provided, and more to experience if only you were privy to their secret. Paul counters this robustly by emphasising the supreme centrality of Christ. He is not a demigod or just one god among many. He is not 'a' means to salvation and redemption; Jesus Christ is God incarnate, his finished work on the cross the only way humankind can be saved from sin, redeemed from its penalties and restored to communion with God. The language we find here is, therefore, unequivocal. Colossians 2:13–15 offers, in my opinion, the best summary of the gospel message.

It is not simply enough just to believe – even in all the correct things. Paul addresses key areas in which we must out-work our salvation. And this does not mean a slavish following of religious rules. Rather, the inner work accomplished through faith in Jesus should be visible to the world. When we clothe ourselves with virtuous characteristics, all our relationships benefit and this ripple effect extends to those who so need to witness – and accept – the power of the gospel.

I pray Paul's words will transform your life.

JANE WALTERS

Reasons to be thankful

We always thank God, the Father of our Lord Jesus Christ, when we pray for you, because we have heard of your faith in Christ Jesus and of the love you have for all God's people – the faith and love that spring from the hope stored up for you in heaven and about which you have already heard in the true message of the gospel that has come to you. In the same way, the gospel is bearing fruit and growing throughout the whole world – just as it has been doing among you since the day you heard it and truly understood God's grace.

'Praying for you', 'Thinking of you', 'Sending warm thoughts' – these are all text messages that friends have sent me at various times. Their short form conveys their heart for me, eliciting a 'That's nice' in response. But they raise further questions: what are you praying? What are you thinking? Why? Tell me more!

Forcibly absent, Paul is communicating to his fellow Christians in the only way he can, and after the preliminary greetings, he dives straight into thanksgiving. This is not just a token 'I'm grateful for you.' His hearers are left in no doubt as to why he is so thankful – and his reasons have much to say to us too.

First, these are people who have put their faith in Jesus. They are both the fruit of his ministry and the seed for future growth. How satisfying it is to hear of their loving response to the gospel! His work was not in vain; his imprisonment no detriment to the spread of the good news. Even from a distance, Paul could witness the effect of their developing faith and the certainty of their future hope.

Second, they are evidence of the truth and vitality of the gospel. The early church was a dynamic, vibrant community of people who had each made a personal commitment, but Pauls' words effectively pan the camera out, moving the focus from individualism to the bigger picture of the gospel spreading far and wide: a glorious creeping vine filled with buds, blossom and potential fruit.

Who are you thankful for today? Bring them to God,
then let them know how much you appreciate them.

JANE WALTERS

Knowing how and why to keep praying

For this reason, since the day we heard about you, we have not stopped praying for you. We continually ask God to fill you with the knowledge of his will through all the wisdom and understanding that the Spirit gives, so that you may live a life worthy of the Lord and please him in every way: bearing fruit in every good work, growing in the knowledge of God, being strengthened with all power according to his glorious might so that you may have great endurance and patience, and giving joyful thanks to the Father, who has qualified you to share in the inheritance of his holy people in the kingdom of light.

Reading through this passage, there is a sense of the Amplified Bible translation about it with almost every point being expanded for emphasis. It is as if Paul wants us to take special note of what he is saying.

Paul's thankfulness for the Colossian believers leads him to pray for them, but listen to how he does it: from the very get-go, unceasingly and continually. What a contrast to our token promises to pray, made so easily and forgotten so quickly. My first response was a justification: of course, Paul can pray like that; what else has he got to do? But this is not him merely trying to use up his free time. He loves these people dearly and wants the very best for them.

Having recently re-read an excellent book on prayer, I have pledged to pray specifically and consistently for some friends in particular need at the moment. Praying daily for the same people brings some challenges. I can almost bore myself with the repetition; I can quickly lose heart at the lack of visible answers. But when we look at Paul's list of prayer points, we notice that these are things we always need – if we are honest enough to admit it.

Are you in need today of God's wisdom? Do you want to live a life that both pleases and glorifies Jesus? Do you need strength and resilience and patience? Ask God to meet your needs, then pray the same things for those you love.

JANE WALTERS

Supremacy of Christ

The Son is the image of the invisible God, the firstborn over all creation. For in him all things were created: things in heaven and on earth, visible and invisible, whether thrones or powers or rulers or authorities; all things have been created through him and for him. He is before all things, and in him all things hold together. And he is the head of the body, the church; he is the beginning and the firstborn from among the dead, so that in everything he might have the supremacy. For God was pleased to have all his fullness dwell in him, and through him to reconcile to himself all things, whether things on earth or things in heaven, by making peace through his blood, shed on the cross.

After church one Sunday, I was talking to River, a troubled woman living locally. She has done the 'Alpha' course but it is fair to say she is not quite there yet, faith-wise. At one point, I asked her, 'But what do you think about Jesus?' She rolled her eyes, replying: 'He's only a *man*. That's the whole problem.' I was keen to redress her lack of understanding, but secretly agreed with part of what she had said. To see Jesus in the wrong way *is* a huge problem, while to view him correctly offers the solution to everything.

Although the church at Colossae was newly established, already the young believers were being swayed by teaching that undermined the lordship of Jesus. When we think along lines that downplays his perfection, his human–divine status or his finished work on the cross, we are on a very slippery slope. If Jesus is not the firstborn over all creation, then he has no rights as Lord. If Jesus is not the embodiment of the fullness of God, then he cannot be our Saviour or even Mediator. If Jesus has not risen from the dead, then not only is he not supreme, he is no better than anyone else. If Jesus is not Lord of all, he is not Lord at all.

Spend some time re-reading the passage, slowly, letting its truths sink into your mind and heart. Let your response be to worship our awesome, wonderful Jesus.

JANE WALTERS

Whiter than white

Once you were alienated from God and were enemies in your minds because of your evil behaviour. But now he has reconciled you by Christ's physical body through death to present you holy in his sight, without blemish and free from accusation – if you continue in your faith, established and firm, and do not move from the hope held out in the gospel. This is the gospel that you heard and that has been proclaimed to every creature under heaven, and of which I, Paul, have become a servant.

If you have ever tried to witness to a non-believer, you will soon discover a major sticking point may be their inflated opinion of themselves: 'I think I'm a pretty decent person'; 'The good I do balances out my mistakes.' And here is one that stopped me in my tracks recently: 'I don't believe my sin gets in the way of me and God.'

Paul does not sugar-coat our condition. Before we accepted the saving work of Jesus and made him Lord of our lives, we were not only distant from God but without the means to bridge the gap. Our sins were not considered on some sort of sliding scale, with none of them ranking particularly terribly. No: we were enemies of God, a fact confirmed hour by hour in our thoughts and deeds (or lack of deeds). Elsewhere in this letter, Paul says that sin has been the spiritual death of us (Colossians 2:13).

Thank God for Jesus! His death has opened the way for us to access the Father, no longer with the stink of sin clinging to us, but clothed in holiness, with not so much as a reminder of who we once were. Imagine one of those implausible clothes-washing adverts, only instead of a mucky T-shirt turning whiter than white, it is our very lives that are transformed. This is no magic trick, but the outworking of the gospel, available to all – a promise you can put to the test.

Spend some time quietly considering what you might have become if Jesus had not called you to him. Confess the sins which bubble up to the surface, then thank him afresh for saving you.

JANE WALTERS

From one who knows

Now I rejoice in what I am suffering for you, and I fill up in my flesh what is still lacking in regard to Christ's afflictions, for the sake of his body, which is the church. I have become its servant by the commission God gave me to present to you the word of God in its fullness – the mystery that has been kept hidden for ages and generations, but is now disclosed to the Lord's people. To them God has chosen to make known among the Gentiles the glorious riches of this mystery, which is Christ in you, the hope of glory. He is the one we proclaim, admonishing and teaching everyone with all wisdom, so that we may present everyone fully mature in Christ. To this end I strenuously contend with all the energy Christ so powerfully works in me.

What captivated your heart when you first heard the gospel? For me, it was the simple message that 'God is love' – I heard it, believed it and staked my entire life on its truth. I cannot imagine responding so enthusiastically to 'knowing God means suffering for his sake', and yet Paul describes this reality with joy.

Throughout this letter, he repeats the theme of fullness, partly to repudiate the claims of the new teachers that the gospel was somehow lacking. Yet, it is a curious choice of phrase, to 'fill up in his flesh' regarding affliction. Did he embrace suffering for Christ's sake (as in Philippians 3:10–11) because of the torment he had inflicted as he persecuted Christians so ruthlessly before his conversion?

Whatever the reason, his testimony was marked by hardship and strenuous exertion, but not because he was striving to attain salvation or favour. Rather, his whole life was a willing demonstration of his godly commission to make Jesus known among both Jews and Gentiles, conveying that we are not just 'in Christ' but Christ is *in us*. Such mystery for our heads to get around, but what joy and hope in our hearts at its truth!

God, we marvel at your ways. Let us never take for granted the gift of grace, that you would choose us for your own. Amen.

JANE WALTERS

Building on solid foundations

So then, just as you received Christ Jesus as Lord, continue to live your lives in him, rooted and built up in him, strengthened in the faith as you were taught, and overflowing with thankfulness. See to it that no one takes you captive through hollow and deceptive philosophy, which depends on human tradition and the elemental spiritual forces of this world rather than on Christ. For in Christ all the fullness of the Deity lives in bodily form, and in Christ you have been brought to fullness. He is the head over every power and authority.

I see two themes in today's passage. The first follows on from yesterday, regarding how being in Christ has established a firm foundation for our lives. If you have ever walked past an abandoned building site, with concrete slabs marking where houses would have been if only the money had not run out, you will know that firm foundations are not enough in themselves. They are designed to be built upon, their depth and span determining the size of the finished structure.

Receiving Christ as Lord is of huge significance, but it is only the first step. The rest of our lives is to be spent gratefully fulfilling his blueprint, enjoying his presence as we do. How tragic it is when we see Christians start to build well, with enthusiasm and vigour, only to veer off-course or abandon their faith altogether.

The second theme centres on Paul's use of the word 'hollow' when thinking of errant teaching, compared to the 'fullness' of knowing Christ. It makes me think of the times I have gorged on so-called empty calories when I am hungry. They might be delicious and moreish and hit the spot for instant gratification, but they offer little by way of nutritional benefit, and before I know it I am hungry all over again. When God offers us fullness – no matter what temptations lie elsewhere – it is no empty promise.

Consider what foundations Christ has laid in your life.
Can you see what has grown up on them during your Christian experience?
Are there any areas left undeveloped or in need of adjustment?
Bring them to him in prayer.

JANE WALTERS

Understanding the finality of Jesus' work

In him you were also circumcised with a circumcision not performed by human hands. Your whole self ruled by the flesh was put off when you were circumcised by Christ, having been buried with him in baptism, in which you were also raised with him through your faith in the working of God, who raised him from the dead. When you were dead in your sins and in the uncircumcision of your flesh, God made you alive with Christ. He forgave us all our sins, having cancelled the charge of our legal indebtedness, which stood against us and condemned us; he has taken it away, nailing it to the cross. And having disarmed the powers and authorities, he made a public spectacle of them, triumphing over them by the cross.

When I first began to consider these verses, I wrote down the following list: complete; decisive; once for all; no half-measures. The effect was extraordinary, like these words enabled me to see the work of redemption in sharper focus. Let us go through Paul's statements and see how you might respond.

Without going into the gritty details, there is nothing half-measured about circumcision. God initiated the ceremony among the Israelites as part of their *permanent* identity as people of God. There could be no sense of 'I used to be a Jew'; it was once and for all. Under the new covenant, there is no requirement for physical circumcision: instead we submit the flesh and its demands to God – and we do not change our mind.

Baptism, likewise, is a definitive ceremony, likened to burial and resurrection here. The old sinful ways are submerged in water and, as the old poster used to put it, a sign is put up saying: 'No fishing!'

But what can be more decisive, more finite, more all-encompassing than the work of Christ on the cross? Our propensity to sin may (woefully) continue but there is no longer any condemnation. Our accuser is silenced. Our Saviour has gloriously triumphed, once and for all.

Spend a few moments thanking God for the finished work of the cross, and pray that he continues to manifest that in your life today.

JANE WALTERS

Living in the shadowlands

Therefore do not let anyone judge you by what you eat or drink, or with regard to a religious festival, a New Moon celebration or a Sabbath day. These are a shadow of the things that were to come; the reality, however, is found in Christ… Since you died with Christ to the elemental spiritual forces of this world, why, as though you still belonged to the world, do you submit to its rules: 'Do not handle! Do not taste! Do not touch!'? These rules, which have to do with things that are all destined to perish with use, are based on merely human commands and teachings. Such regulations indeed have an appearance of wisdom, with their self-imposed worship, their false humility and their harsh treatment of the body, but they lack any value in restraining sensual indulgence.

When a child calls out at night, convinced there are monsters within the shadows, a wise parent brings comfort with a hug and a flick of the light switch. Reality always plays the trump card.

The Old Testament is sometimes described in the New Testament as a shadow: proof that light is present, but not the real thing. Its insistence on keeping the rules was appropriate (and mandatory!) 'back then', but the coming of Jesus changed everything. From Paul's words here, it seems clear that the new teachers were placing undue emphasis not just on Jewish law, but on elements borrowed from paganism. Their message seems to have been a constant 'You're not doing enough; do more.'

Self-discipline and obedience are marks of Christian character and maturity, and Paul is certainly not advocating we throw off restraint. But what is our motivation? If it is fear of punishment, we need to better understand God's loving grace and mercy. Or perhaps it is to show our superiority, or dissatisfaction with scripture, or to imply that God needs a helping hand? Let us leave the shadowlands of rule-keeping and head back to the cross – and quickly – where we find the fulfilment of the law and, in Jesus, true substance and reality.

Lord Jesus, you are enough. Let my active faith and diligent service be motivated by love and bring honour to your name.

JANE WALTERS

Don't be like a cat!

Since, then, you have been raised with Christ, set your hearts on things above, where Christ is, seated at the right hand of God. Set your minds on things above, not on earthly things. For you died, and your life is now hidden with Christ in God. When Christ, who is your life, appears, then you also will appear with him in glory. Put to death, therefore, whatever belongs to your earthly nature: sexual immorality, impurity, lust, evil desires and greed, which is idolatry. Because of these, the wrath of God is coming. You used to walk in these ways, in the life you once lived. But now you must also rid yourselves of all such things as these: anger, rage, malice, slander, and filthy language from your lips.

The title might seem flippant for such serious subject matter, but it is based on verse 7: 'You used to walk in these ways.' When a cat moves house with its owners, it can feel unsettled in its new, unfamiliar territory. Primal instincts drive it to return (sometimes a considerable distance) to the place it feels it belongs.

Before we knew Christ, when we were ignorant of the nature of sin and its consequences, we would not have given a second thought to living as the world does. Just going shopping, we can expect to hear swearing and profanity around us, and to see evidence of anger and greed – all 'normal behaviour' for this day and age. We, however, are not 'normal people': we have been raised with Christ, lifted from the miry pit, up and away from culture's base attitudes and behaviours.

Sometimes the effects of Jesus' lordship of our lives are immediate and transformative: old bad habits disappear, never to return. Sometimes, however, we feel that magnetic pull back to what we once were. It is frustrating and upsetting – for us and those around us – but there is hope. That previous life is not so much 'left behind' as 'dead', despite appearances to the contrary. We no longer have to walk that old path.

Jesus, I want to live to please you. I repent of my sinfulness and ask that you be glorified in and through me. Amen.

JANE WALTERS

Inside and out

Here there is no Gentile or Jew, circumcised or uncircumcised, barbarian, Scythian, slave or free, but Christ is all, and is in all. Therefore, as God's chosen people, holy and dearly loved, clothe yourselves with compassion, kindness, humility, gentleness and patience. Bear with each other and forgive one another if any of you has a grievance against someone. Forgive as the Lord forgave you. And over all these virtues put on love, which binds them all together in perfect unity.

Many years ago, I was taught to always ask what the 'therefore' was there for. Thankfully, it is simple in this case. Yesterday focused on 'putting off' old sinful habits. But we are not left stripped bare; today, we focus on what lovely habits and attitudes to 'put on' instead.

We cannot fail to be reminded of Paul's list of the fruit of the Holy Spirit, found in Galatians 5. There, they are presented as inner qualities that grow naturally from our rootedness in Christ and, similarly to Colossians, follow a set of evil practices we should shun. Here, Paul talks about us donning virtues as an outward expression of our faith.

If this seems superficial, it is worth considering the significance of what we wear. Yes, we may choose some weather- or season-specific clothing regardless of fashion, but usually our clothing choices are based on a desire to express something of our personality. For example, as an extrovert, I love to wear bright colours – even in my hair. If I began wearing beige, not only would I look ill, but it would be at odds with who I was.

Compassion, kindness, humility, gentleness, patience and over-arching love have been the mark of God's holy people since the time he first called them. But it is not enough to lock them away inside our hearts. The world needs to see these demonstrations of God's character. It needs to see our faith and belief system being outworked in ways that run counter to culture.

The next time you forgive someone, it might just be noticed – as surely as my pink fringe.

What challenged you in today's verses?
Are you hiding aspects of your faith? How can that change?

JANE WALTERS

The 'one another' aspect of worship

Let the peace of Christ rule in your hearts, since as members of one body you were called to peace. And be thankful. Let the message of Christ dwell among you richly as you teach and admonish one another with all wisdom through psalms, hymns, and songs from the Spirit, singing to God with gratitude in your hearts. And whatever you do, whether in word or deed, do it all in the name of the Lord Jesus, giving thanks to God the Father through him.

The Covid-19 pandemic turned the world upside-down. Nothing escaped its disruption. When restrictions were finally lifted, for many it marked not a 'return to normal' but a 'new normal', including some Christians no longer regularly attending church. While online services have been a life-saver for the infirm, nothing can beat physically meeting together if and when possible.

These short verses highlight the marvel of fellowship centred on worship and the word. Paul reminds us that we are members of one body – not disparate and detached but essential, connecting parts of a whole. When one is missing, it matters. And these members of one body dwell not just in unity but in peace: something the world fails to offer or achieve in its clubs and societies. Why? Because all we do and are is centred on Christ.

His message is the one upon which we base our lives and try to live out for his glory and witness. His word has the capacity to inform, educate, lead and guide, including challenging our own wisdom and behaviour. We can and must study the Bible on our own, but the corporate aspect brings a greater sense of the fullness that Paul has been teaching in this letter.

Of course, we too can worship on our own – perhaps singing with more gusto when not overheard – but the 'with one another' dimension adds an essential dynamic. When we are flagging, the enthusiastic praise of the person next to us can lift us, reminding us to fix our eyes on Jesus and thank him from the bottom of our hearts.

Spend a few minutes thanking God for those in your church fellowship – and plan to join them if you can, as soon as you can!

JANE WALTERS

63

Specific interactions

Wives, submit yourselves to your husbands, as is fitting in the Lord. Husbands, love your wives and do not be harsh with them. Children, obey your parents in everything, for this pleases the Lord. Fathers, do not embitter your children, or they will become discouraged. Slaves, obey your earthly masters in everything; and do it, not only when their eye is on you and to curry their favour, but with sincerity of heart and reverence for the Lord. Whatever you do, work at it with all your heart, as working for the Lord, not for human masters, since you know that you will receive an inheritance from the Lord as a reward. It is the Lord Christ you are serving.

Today's verses may provoke a strong reaction. Let us ensure, though, that we do not respond with overreaction but allow God to speak and to guide. For there is no more rigorous test of our Christianity than the home setting, where the 'true colours' of our character are revealed. However self-controlled we manage to be when out of the house, back home our guard is lowered. How well do we behave then?

If we are tempted to disregard Paul's teaching as archaic and out of touch, I would issue the challenge to consider it in reverse. What if wives never showed any respect for their husbands? Or if husbands were heartless bullies? What if children refused to accept any authority from the parents, or if parents ruled with an inflexible iron rod? What if workers only bothered doing anything when the boss was actually looking? The result would be anarchy, chaos and the utter breakdown of society.

Instead, we must look to Jesus Christ as our example, viewing our situations through his lens. He was equal with the Father from the beginning yet submitted to his will. He offered himself to others through good works delivered with compassion, respect and dignity. Ultimately, he laid his life down for those who loved him and those who rejected him. Surrendered to God, lovingly available to others: could this be our motto too?

God, help me live among others as you have ordained.
Let me be diligent, respectful and, above all, loving. Amen.

JANE WALTERS

Ready and waiting

Devote yourselves to prayer, being watchful and thankful. And pray for us, too, that God may open a door for our message, so that we may proclaim the mystery of Christ, for which I am in chains. Pray that I may proclaim it clearly, as I should. Be wise in the way you act towards outsiders; make the most of every opportunity. Let your conversation be always full of grace, seasoned with salt, so that you may know how to answer everyone.

Witnessing can feel so tricky, rendering us tongue-tied and impotent, when the most important thing is living out a godly life before a godless society. Today's verses offer hope. Listen to how Paul puts it: 'so that you may know how to answer everyone' (v. 6).

Do you notice the dynamic? Our lifestyle can invite questions about our faith – which we can willingly try to answer.

Let me introduce you to two of my friends. N is a painter who loves working *en plein air*. Passers-by fall easily into conversation with him, provoked sometimes by what is on the canvas. Sometimes, side by side, neither looking directly at each other, a conversation strikes up, going deeper than you might normally expect between strangers. N drops his faith in Jesus into the mix; you can be sure the stranger walks away changed.

D is one of our worship leaders, with a powerful singing ministry. She is also a busker on the streets of our local towns. As she sings her wide variety of tunes, she keeps a close eye on her listeners. On one occasion, she saw a young woman hovering some distance away. D felt prompted to sing a particular track, which proved significant. The woman came over to chat, then they exchanged phone numbers to keep that promising conversation going.

It reminds me of the quote attributed to John Wesley: 'I set myself on fire and people come to watch me burn.' Living a Christ-centred life will provoke reaction. Let us be ready with our wisdom and grace-filled responses.

If someone asked you about your faith, would you know what to say?
Try writing out a short testimony so that you can be prepared
next time someone asks.

JANE WALTERS

Preparing for legacy

Epaphras, who is one of you and a servant of Christ Jesus, sends greetings. He is always wrestling in prayer for you, that you may stand firm in all the will of God, mature and fully assured. I vouch for him that he is working hard for you and for those at Laodicea and Hierapolis. Our dear friend Luke, the doctor, and Demas send greetings... Tell Archippus: 'See to it that you complete the ministry you have received in the Lord.' I, Paul, write this greeting in my own hand. Remember my chains. Grace be with you.

It is worth reading all of this final section (verses 7–18) to fully appreciate the warmth of these personal greetings. Paul's objective, his teaching on Christ's centrality and the true gospel, has been met. But there is space for more: the encouragement and appreciation of those among whom he serves.

The letter began with reference to Epaphras (Colossian 1:7), and he gets a special mention at the end. We know that he came from the Colossae area, was converted under Paul's ministry and was now helping to establish the church there. His devotion is evident: wrestling in prayer – much as his mentor, Paul, had demonstrated.

I wonder if we consider the idea of legacy in our own serving areas? Sometimes we are so absorbed in our current tasks and responsibilities that there is little capacity to look ahead. Perhaps we feel our own burdens so keenly that the thought of passing on the baton seems irrelevant or even impossible. Heaven forbid we believe we are irreplaceable!

Epaphras, like fellow mentee Timothy, was born again and nurtured through Paul in order that he could develop a ministry that went further than Paul was able to take it. Imagine what would have happened if he had not. Unable to be physically present, Paul's chains would have bound the progress of the gospel. Through willing co-workers, though, its transforming power continues to spread.

Pray for those who come after you, or someone within your church, that God would prepare them ahead of their appointing.

JANE WALTERS

God the avenger: Psalms 73—78

When I was invited to write on these psalms, I had a feeling I had written on them before. It turned out that I have written on them twice before in the past 20 years! However, they still repay further close study.

These worship songs introduce the third book of Psalms, and are written by the music leader Asaph rather than by King David. They therefore relate more to events in the life of God's people and occasionally the life of the psalmist, rather than to incidents in David's tumultuous life.

I have chosen the title 'God the avenger' not because they portray God as in any way vengeful. I was thinking more of the stylish 1960s TV spy series *The Avengers*, in which Patrick Macnee as John Steed and Honor Blackman as Cathy Gale/Diana Rigg as Emma Peel served the cause of justice and caught villains attacking the state. The God of these psalms swoops in to rescue God's people from enemies who threaten them, either from outside or within. The psalms hint at the prophets' promise that one day, all oppression will be overcome and humanity will live once more in a world of peace and plenty.

When reading psalms (and prophecy) we need always to remember that they are poetry, although we do not have space to set them out that way here. Hebrew poetry uses a form in which the second line of a verse echoes the first line using different words and images; for instance: 'But as for me, my feet had almost stumbled; my steps had nearly slipped' (Psalm 73:2, NRSV). Also, as with all poetry, much of what is said is metaphorical; for example: 'Therefore pride is their necklace; violence covers them like a garment' (v. 6). We will get more out of these ancient songs if we look out for these features.

It might also be helpful to compare them with our modern worship songs or indeed our traditional hymns. The psalms are not afraid to address events that are happening in the world around – they go well beyond what has sometimes been caricatured as 'me and God, God and me'. How might our worship face the needy world and not just our own feelings?

VERONICA ZUNDEL

Appearances can be deceptive

Truly God is good to Israel, to those who are pure in heart. But as for me, my feet had almost stumbled; my steps had nearly slipped. For I was envious of the arrogant; I saw the prosperity of the wicked. For they have no pain; their bodies are sound and sleek. They are not in trouble as others are; they are not plagued like other people. Therefore pride is their necklace; violence covers them like a garment.

Twenty-four years after I graduated, I went to my first college reunion. There I met a woman who had been one of my closest friends at university, but with whom I had lost touch. She was slim, tanned and elegantly dressed; she had a beloved husband, two adult children who had both achieved firsts at Oxford, and a house in France; she lectured in law and in nutrition; and she did not look a day older than when I had last seen her at graduation. I was green with envy, which is my greatest weakness.

Two years later, I saw her at another reunion and observed that she looked noticeably older. As we talked, I found out that since we last met, her daughter, in her early 20s, had been killed in a car crash. I vowed immediately never to envy anyone again – a vow I have not entirely kept, but when I do succumb to envy I remember her and it brings me up short.

My friend was not 'the wicked' described in these verses; indeed, she had a real faith in God. But we never know what may happen in life. We should not assume that others have it all and we do not. When we see people's happy family pictures on social media or read of their or their children's successes, we need to remember that what we see is only the surface. Those who do evil may prosper, those who do good may suffer, but God is bringing in a great reversal, in which, in Mary's words, 'He has brought down the powerful from their thrones and lifted up the lowly' (Luke 1:52). So certain is Mary of this that she puts it in the past, not future tense.

'Blessed are those who mourn, for they will be comforted'
(Matthew 5:4).

VERONICA ZUNDEL

Who cares?

Therefore the people turn and praise them and find no fault in them. And they say, 'How can God know? Is there knowledge in the Most High?' Such are the wicked; always at ease, they increase in riches. All in vain I have kept my heart clean and washed my hands in innocence. For all day long I have been plagued and am punished every morning.

Do you watch television or read magazines and see celebrities who seem utterly shallow? Or see the news and find politicians who pursue obviously evil or uncaring policies, and yet have millions of supporters? Last year we had a general election in the UK, and other major elections have happened in many countries around the world since, not least in the USA. Do we choose leaders who prioritise the poor, vulnerable and oppressed, or those who are clearly in office to line their own pockets and those of their rich friends?

Humans are built to worship, and if we do not worship God (and even sometimes if we do!), we will worship money, sex, power, or charismatic leaders or performers. There is nothing wrong in admiring those who are accomplished. There is nothing inherently wrong in money, which can be shared, or in sex, reinforcing a lifelong relationship, or in power as 'power to' do good rather than 'power over' others. However, they all have a way of taking us over and dominating our lives, unless we surrender them to God, who knows how to use them best.

If, however, we have done our best to follow Jesus, and still our lives seem like a constant burden and maybe even unbearable, we may want to echo the psalmist's 'All in vain'. Is it worth it? When, if ever, will we get our promised reward?

The psalmist will get his answer in tomorrow's reading. In the meantime, remember that in the hardest life there are glimpses of joy – the satisfaction of knowing we have done the right thing, the warmth of fellowship with those we travel with, the beauty of creation, of children, of innocent animals.

'But this I call to mind, and therefore I have hope: The steadfast love of the Lord never ceases, his mercies never come to an end' (Lamentations 3:21–22).

VERONICA ZUNDEL

The illusion of success

If I had said, 'I will talk on in this way,' I would have been untrue to the circle of your children. But when I thought how to understand this, it seemed to me a wearisome task, until I went into the sanctuary of God; then I perceived their end. Truly you set them in slippery places; you make them fall to ruin. How they are destroyed in a moment, swept away utterly by terrors! They are like a dream when one awakes; on awaking you despise their phantoms.

Our new cat has commandeered the chair in which I have habitually sat to pray for over 40 years. She curls up and sleeps there in the mornings and I need to find another sanctuary! 'Sanctuary' can have a number of meanings. It could be a physical place, time or attitude: the temple, synagogue, church, a retreat house, time to get away and reflect, or simply a way of withdrawing into our own soul to commune with God.

How does a place or time like this offer the writer of this psalm a different view on the apparent unfairness of life? I think there might be a clue in verse 15: 'I would have been untrue to the circle of your children.' In worship, we (ideally) encounter other people who live by a different set of values, even when they cost everything.

In carving out time for God, we gain a fresh perspective, in which the flourishing of those who do not seem to deserve their good fortune turns out to be very temporary and fragile. When God judges, what matters is not our wealth, fame, achievements or even plain good luck. What matters is whether we have been faithful, kind, self-sacrificing, generous. By 'entering the sanctuary' we rediscover that 'the race is not to the swift, nor the battle to the strong… but time and chance happen to them all' (Ecclesiastes 9:11).

'Now if anyone builds on the foundation with gold, silver, precious stones, wood, hay, straw – the work of each builder will become visible, for the day will disclose it, because it will be revealed with fire, and the fire will test what sort of work each has done' (1 Corinthians 3:12–13).

VERONICA ZUNDEL

Jesus, remember me

O God, why do you cast us off forever? Why does your anger smoke against the sheep of your pasture? Remember your congregation, which you acquired long ago, which you redeemed to be the tribe of your heritage. Remember Mount Zion, where you came to dwell. Direct your steps to the perpetual ruins; the enemy has destroyed everything in the sanctuary. Your foes have roared within your holy place; they set up their emblems there. At the upper entrance they hacked the wooden trellis with axes. And then, with hatchets and hammers, they smashed all its carved work.

Day after day on television we see the effect of war on daily life. Homes, schools, hospitals demolished, standing roofless, windowless, scorched and shattered. In this psalm, even the beautiful temple, location of so much hope and prayer, is smashed to pieces. The place where, in the previous psalm, the writer went for new insight, is gone.

Where Psalm 73 expressed an individual sorrow, this one expresses a national one. I think of the state of Europe after World War II, with bomb sites remaining for decades – 'perpetual ruins'. The psalmist has no hesitation in attributing this situation to God; God has allowed the enemy to triumph because of the disobedience of God's people. We might have difficulties with this approach today. Jesus himself said, when his disciples asked him about the link between sin and suffering: 'Those eighteen who were killed when the tower of Siloam fell on them – do you think that they were worse offenders than all the others living in Jerusalem?' (Luke 13:4).

The psalmist's response, however, is not to plead for forgiveness. Rather, he exhorts God to remember: remember the people God chose, remember the place where God asked to be honoured. Do we ever pray like this? We have so much more of which to remind God than Asaph had – God's coming among us in Jesus, his life and teaching, his sacrificial death and resurrection. It is not that God forgets, it is that by praying this way, we remember that God does, indeed, remember us.

'See, I have inscribed you on the palms of my hands;
your walls are continually before me' (Isaiah 49:16).

VERONICA ZUNDEL

Help, Lord!

Yet God my King is from of old, working salvation in the earth. You divided the sea by your might; you broke the heads of the dragons in the waters... Yours is the day, yours also the night; you established the luminaries and the sun... Remember this, O Lord, how the enemy scoffs, and an impious people reviles your name. Do not deliver the soul of your dove to the wild animals; do not forget the life of your poor forever. Have regard for your covenant, for the dark places of the land are full of the haunts of violence.

One day last year I went with my husband to sign lasting powers of attorney for each other, and to establish our son as replacement attorney should both of us become incapable. We trust each other to make good decisions on each other's behalf, but these legal documents are a kind of covenant which puts that trust into a binding form. As I write this, it is election day, and whoever wins, they enter a covenant to govern to the best of their ability, and we have the right to recall them to their promises.

In the Old Testament, God makes covenants with humankind, beginning with the 'rainbow covenant' with Noah and all the succeeding human race, and going on to the covenant with the chosen people through Abraham. So here Asaph continues his project of reminding God of God's obligations, beginning with the fact that God rules over creation in both exceptional circumstances (dragons in the waters) and everyday phenomena (day and night, sun and stars). He also points out to God how violence has turned the good creation into a collection of 'dark places'.

God knows all this, of course; but the psalmist needs to express his fear and concern. A good parent may know very well what her child needs; but she still delights in hearing the child ask for it, and the request strengthens the bond between child and parent. Prayer is more than just requests, it is praise, thankfulness, confession, repentance; but perhaps nothing builds our relationship with God more than asking for help and getting it.

'Then Jesus, crying with a loud voice, said,
"Father, into your hands I commend my spirit"' (Luke 23:46).

VERONICA ZUNDEL

Justice will come

We give thanks to you, O God; we give thanks; your name is near. People tell of your wondrous deeds. At the set time that I appoint, I will judge with equity. When the earth totters, with all its inhabitants, it is I who keep its pillars steady. I say to the boastful, 'Do not boast,' and to the wicked, 'Do not lift up your horn; do not lift up your horn on high or speak with insolent neck.'

Hitler, by whose policies all my mother's family were murdered, boasted that he would establish a 'thousand year Reich (kingdom)'. In the event, he managed just twelve years before, losing the war and despairing, he shot himself in a bunker. The 'horn' in biblical passages like this one signifies the boasts of the powerful, and the 'insolent neck' the pride these are based on (a concept which still survives in our phrase 'sheer brass neck').

This psalm probably commemorates a victory over the nation's enemies, and it re-establishes that it is God, not military powers, who ultimately preserves the earth and judges its inhabitants. That there will finally be justice in the world is one of God's greatest promises and fuels many people's faith.

We only have to look around to see how broken our world is, and we long for someone to fix it. In the end, this task is beyond politicians, social workers, educationalists or 'influencers', because we are all fallible humans working in constrained circumstances. Only God can complete this task, and today we hear God's voice saying this will happen, 'At the set time that I appoint' (v. 2). Speculation about the end times is a waste of energy; cultivating patience and hope for the kingdom a far more fruitful exercise.

There are many times in human life when apparently 'the earth totters' – whether this is an actual earthquake or a family crisis. I'm sure the psalmist did not actually believe the globe had pillars: this is a poetic image to convey the stabilising power of God. A psalm to remember when everything seems to be falling apart.

'The kingdom of the world has become the kingdom of our Lord and of his Messiah, and he will reign forever and ever' (Revelation 11:15).

VERONICA ZUNDEL

A cup of justice

For not from the east or from the west and not from the wilderness comes lifting up, but it is God who executes judgement, putting down one and lifting up another. For in the hand of the Lord there is a cup with foaming wine, well mixed; he will pour a draught from it, and all the wicked of the earth shall drain it down to the dregs. But I will rejoice forever; I will sing praises to the God of Jacob. All the horns of the wicked I will cut off, but the horns of the righteous shall be exalted.

A cup of foaming wine from the hand of God sounds to us like a pleasing prospect. But this cup, as often in the Old Testament, is a poisoned chalice: it signifies punishment, a cup the drinker is reluctant to swallow. This is where our theme of 'God the avenger' really comes into focus: 'the wicked' are those who exploit and oppress the vulnerable, and it is fitting that they should receive the penalty for this.

Some would use this to say the God of the Old Testament is a punitive, judgemental God, while it is only in the New Testament that God becomes merciful. This is far from the truth. The Old Testament is packed with references to God's infinite mercy and compassion. Consider these words from Psalm 103: 'The Lord is merciful and gracious, slow to anger and abounding in steadfast love. He will not always accuse, nor will he keep his anger forever. He does not deal with us according to our sins, nor repay us according to our iniquities' (Psalm 103:8–10).

God's 'vengeance' is not a spiteful, tit-for-tat response, but the triumph of justice over injustice. The biblical God is a judge, not a Mafia boss! This is about restoring the balance of creation, putting down those who have become over-powerful and raising up those who are weak. We return again to Mary's great prophectic song: 'He has shown strength with his arm; he has scattered the proud in the imagination of their hearts' (Luke 1:51). Jesus has drunk the cup for us, freeing us from judgement.

'Father, if you are willing, remove this cup from me,
yet not my will but yours be done' (Luke 22:42).

VERONICA ZUNDEL

God's disarmament plan

In Judah God is known; his name is great in Israel. His abode has been established in Salem, his dwelling place in Zion. There he broke the flashing arrows, the shield, the sword, and the weapons of war. Glorious are you, more majestic than the everlasting mountains. The courageous were stripped of their spoil; they sank into sleep; none of the troops was able to lift a hand. At your rebuke, O God of Jacob, both rider and horse lay stunned.

Since 2023, two wars in particular – in Gaza and Ukraine – have been making the news, but there are many more conflicts around the world that are claiming the lives of innocent children, mothers and fathers, grandparents, nurses, doctors. I wonder how it feels to read these verses in the context of one of those wars, rather than in the safety that most of us are reading them? What does it mean to those who are suffering under shelling, losing their homes, schools and hospitals, to read that God 'broke the flashing arrows, the shield, the sword and the weapons of war' (v. 3) and translate this into today's much more powerful weaponry?

One thing it can definitely mean is that we cannot take pride in 'winning' a war. Throughout the Old Testament it is made clear that only God wins wars, that victory is based not in superior strength or weaponry but only in God's choice to defend God's people. It is notable here that God's victory comes not by greater violence but by breaking the weapons and stunning the soldiers.

As Christians we follow the Prince of Peace, who 'makes wars cease to the end of the earth' (Psalm 46:9). This is both a promise and a challenge: if ending wars is the work of God, why are God's people, who are meant to imitate God, not doing more of it? This is a complex issue, of course, and we can debate the how and the when – but surely not the why. We cannot kill in God's name when God is the one whose mission is to end the killing.

---

*'Then Jesus said to him, "Put your sword back into its place,
for all who take the sword will die by the sword"' (Matthew 26:52).*

VERONICA ZUNDEL

Shock and awe

But you indeed are awesome! Who can stand before you when once your anger is roused? From the heavens you uttered judgement; the earth feared and was still when God rose up to establish judgement, to save all the oppressed of the earth. Human wrath serves only to praise you, when you bind the last bit of your wrath around you. Make vows to the Lord your God and perform them; let all who are around him bring gifts to the one who is awesome, who cuts off the spirit of princes, who inspires fear in the kings of the earth.

When did you last experience real awe? Chances are it was at some natural phenomenon – Niagara Falls, for example, or an erupting volcano; but we can also experience awe at the birth of a baby or even at the 'good death' of a person who has lived a long and faithful life. 'Awesome' has become a bit overused these days: anything from a rock concert to a restaurant meal can be 'awesome'.

God's 'awesomeness' here is something that causes the earth to fall silent in wonder – as surely we all would, if we suddenly found all wars had ceased around the world and that all the oppressed were liberated. Even human anger, the source of so much pain and destruction, turns into praise of God when we see the results of God's righteous anger, which is not destructive but creates justice. I often think of God's 'wrath' as a bit like the anger of a mother when she finds her child who has been lost in a crowded place – she is not really angry at the child, she is just expressing her feelings of anger that the child was lost and relief at finding them.

How should we respond to the acts of this awesome God? In an Old Testament context this might mean giving a special sacrifice at the temple or tabernacle – no small gift when you consider how vital livestock and grain were to people's survival. Now God wants different gifts: 'present your bodies as a living sacrifice' (Romans 12:1). Our daily lives, lived in love and faithfulness, are our offering.

'Although he was a Son, he learned obedience through what he suffered'
(Hebrews 5:8).

VERONICA ZUNDEL

Godforsaken

I cry aloud to God, aloud to God, that he may hear me. In the day of my trouble I seek the Lord; in the night my hand is stretched out without wearying; my soul refuses to be comforted. I think of God, and I moan; I meditate, and my spirit faints. You keep my eyelids from closing; I am so troubled that I cannot speak. I consider the days of old and remember the years of long ago. I commune with my heart in the night; I meditate and search my spirit: 'Will the Lord spurn forever and never again be favourable?'

In any year in the UK, one in four people will experience a mental health problem. At the same time, everyone will suffer bereavement at some point, and many people will encounter relationship problems, trouble at work (or trouble through lack of work), money difficulties or physical ill health in themselves or a loved one. As M. Scott Peck says right at the beginning of his 1978 bestseller *The Road Less Traveled*: 'Life is difficult'.

We do not know what has caused the psalmist such anxiety and fear. Yet he does not turn away from God as a result, but rather turns to God in honesty and in search of comfort. The problem with the false teaching that God will give us constant joy is that when this is not the reality, people who have believed it may conclude that God is either not there or does not care, and give up on their faith. One of the things I love about the Mennonite church is that because their ancestors were persecuted by Roman Catholics and Protestants, they had to develop an adequate theology of suffering. It seems to me that the promise of Jesus most completely fulfilled is: 'In the world you will have trouble' (John 16:33, NEB).

What I like about this psalm is how frankly the writer spills out his heart to God. There is no attempt to disguise how bad he is feeling. He asks the hard questions: has God turned away from him, or from God's people? If you do not ask the questions, you will never get the answers.

'My God, my God, why have you forsaken me?'
(Matthew 27:46, quoting Psalm 22:1)

VERONICA ZUNDEL

God of power, God of weakness

I will call to mind the deeds of the Lord; I will remember your wonders of old… When the waters saw you, O God, when the waters saw you, they were afraid; the very deep trembled. The clouds poured out water; the skies thundered; your arrows flashed on every side. The crash of your thunder was in the whirlwind; your lightnings lit up the world; the earth trembled and shook. Your way was through the sea, your path through the mighty waters, yet your footprints were unseen. You led your people like a flock by the hand of Moses and Aaron.

Are you a storm chaser or a storm hater? I love to watch a good thunderstorm from the safety of my window; I am not so sure about being out in it! The psalmist sees God's presence in natural phenomena: crashing storms, perhaps even earthquakes or volcanoes. He then makes an immediate link to God leading the Israelites out of slavery in Egypt. The implication seems to be that if God can show such power in the world of nature, how much more power can God show in rescuing us from danger and sorrow?

Is this why so often in history the power of God has been embraced by those who were most powerless? This is still true in some parts of the world, but in the affluent west and north, most of us have so much power ourselves that we think we have no need of a mighty God. Perhaps this is where we need to rediscover the powerless God, who in Jesus hung on the cross and submitted to death. In finding this powerless God we will also become aware of the powerless among us, even in the wealthiest society: the asylum seeker, the worker trapped in modern slavery, the single mother trying to survive on benefits in run-down housing.

If we find this perspective, then we will also remember the history of God, through God's people, saving the poor and the helpless, and we will engage in this rescuing work ourselves, with the help of God and each other. It may not be dramatic, but we may find ourselves performing small wonders.

'My grace is sufficient for you, for power is made perfect in weakness'
(2 Corinthians 12:9).

VERONICA ZUNDEL

The past: good example or awful warning?

Give ear, O my people, to my teaching; incline your ears to the words of my mouth. I will open my mouth in a parable; I will utter dark sayings from of old, things that we have heard and known, that our ancestors have told us… He established a decree in Jacob and appointed a law in Israel, which he commanded our ancestors to teach to their children… so that they should set their hope in God, and not forget the works of God, but keep his commandments; and that they should not be like their ancestors, a stubborn and rebellious generation, a generation whose heart was not steadfast, whose spirit was not faithful to God.

'It wasn't like this in my day' is one of the most frequent complaints of older people (like myself). No, it was not – it was in many ways a great deal worse! Less than a century ago, children were dying of preventable diseases (they still are in the developing world), corporal punishment was permitted, poverty was rife, abuse of all kinds was swept under the carpet. We do not always appreciate how progress has benefited us.

    This psalm contains a contradiction. At one moment the writer is telling people to teach their children the commands of God, just as their ancestors taught them, and at the next he is saying the point is that they should not be like their ancestors, who broke those same commandments! The core message here is that we should do all we can to teach our children the values we live by and the love of God who has given us these values. But this is not just for the sake of the next generation knowing all about our faith. It is so that they will 'keep [God's] commandments' (v. 7).

    My husband and I have not succeeded in keeping our son in the Christian faith. But I am happy to see that he still has the values of loyalty, generosity, kindness and love that have been instilled in him from childhood. Perhaps one day, when he finds he needs extra strength to maintain those values, he will come back to God.

'This people honours me with their lips, but their hearts are far from me'
(Matthew 15:8, quoting Isaiah 29:13).

VERONICA ZUNDEL

A forgiven people

Their heart was not steadfast towards him; they were not true to his covenant. Yet he, being compassionate, forgave their iniquity and did not destroy them; often he restrained his anger and did not stir up all his wrath. He remembered that they were but flesh, a wind that passes and does not come again.

'Then Peter came and said to him, "Lord, if my brother or sister sins against me, how often should I forgive? As many as seven times?"' (Matthew 18:21). Peter no doubt thought he was being very generous. Seven was a significant number, the number of completeness. Surely that would be enough? But: 'Jesus said to him, "Not seven times, but, I tell you, seventy-seven times"' (v. 22; in some versions, 'seventy times seven').

How can we reach that exalted level of forgiveness? I for one find it difficult even to forgive once. Psalm 78, a psalm of remembering, gives us the answer. Yesterday we remembered God's commandments and our own failure to live up to them. Today the psalmist remembers how often God forgave God's people, made concessions to their human frailty and mended their relationship with God when it had been broken from their side. It is in the context of God's forgiveness of us, as so many of Jesus' parables show, that we can be free to forgive others.

There is a virtuous circle at work here: it is only if we forgive others that we can experience God's forgiveness of us: 'And forgive us our debts, as we also have forgiven our debtors' (Matthew 6:12). But also, we can only extend this forgiveness if we understand how much God has forgiven us.

I find that the older I get, the more I am aware of my own failings and weaknesses. I also become more aware of the many evils that are done in God's name! The people of God have never been a perfect people; the best we can do is to become more conscious of our own imperfections, and of how much God loves us anyway.

'Father, forgive them, for they do not know what they are doing'
(Luke 23:34).

VERONICA ZUNDEL

Miniature Old Testament

Then the Lord awoke as from sleep, like a warrior shouting because of wine. He put his adversaries to rout; he put them to everlasting disgrace... He built his sanctuary like the high heavens, like the earth, which he has founded forever. He chose his servant David and took him from the sheepfolds; from tending the nursing ewes he brought him to be the shepherd of his people Jacob, of Israel, his inheritance. With upright heart he tended them and guided them with skilful hand.

Two years ago my Methodist church celebrated its 200th anniversary with a series of celebratory events. They also published a book on the church's history, full of photographs and reminiscences about the church's life and mission, especially its work among children and young people, and its creativity through drama and art. I proofread the final version, and it was an inspiring read, though it made me wish I had discovered this congregation earlier, in its 'glory days'!

The book of Psalms has been called 'the Old Testament in miniature', and some longer psalms do indeed recount the whole history of God's people so far. Psalm 78 is one of these: essentially it is a history of God's people in the promised land, of their repeated failures to live up to their calling, and of how in spite of this God gave them victory over those who wanted to destroy them.

It should not be used to justify any actions of the modern secular state of Israel, which is a different entity. No Israeli prime minister is King David, whose leadership is praised here. Indeed, we should always be careful when applying the scriptures to modern politics. We need to ask God's Spirit to guide us in identifying the good and condemning the bad.

Yet we can still be grateful when we have good, consistent leadership in church or state. Ultimately, though, we are all dependent on God for our safety and stability. What this series of psalms has told us is that God is the source of all justice and equity. If we want a good society, we need people who find their values in Jesus and who practise them faithfully.

'You are the salt of the earth... you are the light of the world'
(Matthew 5:13–14).

VERONICA ZUNDEL

Jonah, the reluctant prophet

Jonah's story demonstrates an acute understanding of human frailties. We probably think we know the story well; many of us will remember from childhood the story of a man being thrown overboard into stormy waters and being swallowed up by a whale. But this is only one element in a short yet dense examination of the relationship between God and humanity. Jonah is an Everyman, a very ordinary character who is tasked with something difficult and does his best to avoid doing it. He ducks and twists, trying to hide from God, although this proves to be a fruitless endeavour as God demonstrates a determined commitment to the whole of creation.

Jonah, when asked who he is, describes himself as 'a Hebrew' who worships 'the God of heaven'. This identity does not, however, permeate his whole being; he likes to categorise himself as a member of a faith community while being reluctant to live in a way that is congruent with the religion he professes to follow. It is those around Jonah who are not conventionally 'religious' – the sailors who throw him into the sea and the wicked inhabitants of Nineveh – who are shown to be more theologically inclined than the prophet himself. The sailors agonise about their actions and are respectful of Jonah's God, while the citizens of Nineveh immediately grasp the implications of their behaviour. In this story, there are 'insiders' and 'outsiders', but all matter to God and all are given opportunities – as is Jonah – to change their ways.

The book of Jonah reads like a story without a conventional beginning or end. We are pitched into the action without any preamble – '*Now* the word of the Lord came to Jonah…' (Jonah 1:1, NRSV) – and the abrupt final sentence leaves God's words hanging in the air. 'Should I not care?' asks God, but we do not find out how Jonah responds. This encourages us to consider not only how Jonah might react at this point, but also wonder what we would do if we were faced with a similar situation. It is Jonah's flaws and frailties that make him an entertaining companion; simultaneously he holds up a mirror in which we can see our own reflection. To journey with him is to discover ourselves.

AMANDA BLOOR

Help!

Now the word of the Lord came to Jonah son of Amittai, saying, 'Go at once to Nineveh, that great city, and cry out against it, for their wickedness has come up before me.' But Jonah set out to flee to Tarshish from the presence of the Lord. He went down to Joppa and found a ship going to Tarshish; so he paid his fare and went on board.

There's a lovely combination in this passage of the marvellous and the mundane. 'Go and do this,' says God, and instead of considering the request or even of arguing with God ('What, me? Surely not!'), Jonah rushes to the coast and buys the equivalent of a ticket on the number 6 bus. It is not the usual reaction of a prophet entrusted with a significant undertaking.

And what God has commanded is not straightforward. Instead of going to talk to an individual, perhaps a significant figure in the community, to pass on God's word, Jonah has been told to 'cry out' against a whole city. Where do you start with such a task?

It is comically naive of Jonah to believe that if God can find him to issue that order, getting on a boat with other passengers will render him anonymous. But we can probably feel sympathy for someone who finds, out of the blue, God speaking to him in such uncompromising terms. We might well, if we were in that position, want to run away.

I wonder if there has been a time in your life when your instinct was that something was being demanded of you that felt beyond your capabilities? Jonah's mistake was to believe that the job he had been given had to be completed in his own strength. If he had been able to trust that God would be in it, his response might have been very different.

God of all knowledge and power, give me the grace to know that you will never ask more of me than I am able to achieve with your help. Be with me, enable me and build me up so that I can always respond with 'Yes.' Amen.

AMANDA BLOOR

Desperate times and desperate measures

Such a mighty storm came upon the sea that the ship threatened to break up. Then the sailors were afraid, and each cried to his god… Jonah, meanwhile, had gone down into the hold of the ship and had lain down and was fast asleep. The captain came and said to him, 'What are you doing sound asleep? Get up; call on your god! Perhaps the god will spare us a thought so that we do not perish.'

There's a well-known saying that there are no atheists in foxholes; that is, when in positions of extreme danger and all other options have failed, even the apparently faithless can find themselves turning to God. We see that happening here. The sailors have thrown their cargo overboard to lighten the ship, but they know that they are in mortal peril. Prayer to their own gods has had no impact, but in desperation they will try anything. Shaking the exhausted Jonah awake, the captain orders him to pray to his own god; perhaps that will work. What do they have to lose?

Interestingly, we are not told if Jonah did get on his knees, as the story moves on in another direction. I wonder if his faith was still strong enough to cause him to plead for rescue, or if, ashamed at his cowardice, he was convinced that he was unworthy to even approach God in prayer?

It can be all too easy to believe that we are too insignificant or too sinful to deserve God's attention, but that is to undermine all that Jesus has done for us. We matter to God, not because we have earned attention, but because we are loved. Paul suggested, in his first letter to the Thessalonians, that we should 'pray without ceasing' (1 Thessalonians 5:17). That's a good precept to live by at all times, not only in desperate moments.

Gracious God, whose Son Jesus Christ taught us the depths of your love, help us to know that we can always come to you in prayer. Let us trust that we are welcomed and heard. Give us the strength we need to face troubles and the joy of knowing that we matter to you. Amen.

AMANDA BLOOR

You have rescued me

They picked Jonah up and threw him into the sea, and the sea ceased from its raging. Then the men feared the Lord even more, and they offered a sacrifice to the Lord and made vows. But the Lord provided a large fish to swallow up Jonah, and Jonah was in the belly of the fish for three days and three nights. Then Jonah prayed to the Lord his God from the belly of the fish.

It is easy to believe, when things go badly wrong, that God is angry and is punishing us. That is clearly what Jonah thought when a great storm arose, threatening everyone's lives. Knowing that he was running away from God, he could only think of one thing to do – to encourage the crew to cast him over the side of the boat. Perhaps then, God's vengeance would be wreaked solely on the fugitive prophet rather than those sailing with him.

Although the sailors themselves were initially repulsed by the idea of sending a man to certain death in the raging waters, they seemed to have no other option. As they watched, it must have seemed as if God was wreaking vengeance upon Jonah by ensuring a grisly and memorable death. Surely this was a warning to all? But as the story unfolds, it becomes clear that the fish is a means of rescue, a somewhat unorthodox shelter from stormy waters. God does not want Jonah to die; rather Jonah is rescued and given time to reflect and to pray.

If Jonah, in all his weakness, matters this much to God, then we should remember that we also matter. God understands our failings and is sympathetic to our needs. Jonah's rescue reminds us that moments of apparent disaster are those times when we need God most. Like Jonah, we have the opportunity to accept God's offer of shelter from the storm and pray – wherever we find ourselves.

When storms are raging, Lord, and I feel that things are out of control, help me to remember that you love me still. Give me a place of shelter, so that in quietness I can draw close to you, for you are my help and my salvation. Amen.

AMANDA BLOOR

Remembering the Lord

'You brought up my life from the Pit, O Lord my God. As my life was ebbing away, I remembered the Lord, and my prayer came to you, into your holy temple. Those who worship vain idols forsake their true loyalty. But I with the voice of thanksgiving will sacrifice to you; what I have vowed I will pay. Deliverance belongs to the Lord!' Then the Lord spoke to the fish, and it vomited Jonah out onto the dry land.

A near-death experience for Jonah leads to a new commitment to obedience and faithfulness. 'What I have vowed, I will pay,' he promises. It is worth noting that this promise comes before Jonah's return to the safety of dry land; this prayer is not a transaction – 'If you do *this*, God, then I'll do *that*.' Rather, it is a statement of belief and dedication. Jonah surrenders himself totally to God and trusts that he will be saved.

The fact that after this the fish vomits up Jonah on to a nearby beach appears to be less significant than the act of faith and loyalty that precedes it. In that moment of prayer and self-giving, Jonah seems to have found peace. Of course he is hoping to be saved from what feels like rapidly approaching death – the struggle to live is an overriding human instinct – but he also remembers all that the Lord has done for him, all that is really important. As his life is 'ebbing away', Jonah's thoughts turn to God.

Sometimes it is in life's most difficult moments, as we are forced to re-examine our lives and re-evaluate what matters most, that the way ahead can become a little bit clearer. In darkness, even a tiny pinprick of light can shine out. Perhaps we can think of moments in our own lives when our choice has been to struggle and rail against the inevitable or to look for Christ's guiding light and loving presence. Like Jonah, we can hope in times of trouble to remember the Lord.

Darkness sometimes threatens to overwhelm me, Lord,
but you are my hope and my salvation. You are light in darkness,
hope against despair. Let my prayers always come to you. Amen.

AMANDA BLOOR

Hearing the news

Now Nineveh was an exceedingly large city, a three days' walk across. Jonah began to go into the city, going a day's walk. And he cried out, 'Forty days more, and Nineveh shall be overthrown!' And the people of Nineveh believed God; they proclaimed a fast, and everyone, great and small, put on sackcloth. When the news reached the king of Nineveh, he rose from his throne, removed his robe, covered himself with sackcloth, and sat in ashes.

I find that in today's multimedia society, where rapidly changing information is thrown at us from a multiplicity of sources throughout the day, it can be difficult to recognise what is important and what is trivial, inaccurate or sensationalist. As a result, I can simply switch off and stop taking notice. The risk is, of course, that I then miss something that I really need to know.

Jonah's proclamation of disaster could well have been dismissed or ignored by the citizens of Nineveh, because it told harsh truths. Instead, they took him seriously and quickly responded in the best way they could; they demonstrated their submission to God by fasting and wearing the simplest garments as signs of repentance. Even the king humbled himself by dressing in sackcloth and sitting in ashes. Nineveh became a place of mourning and guilty recognition of wrongdoing. I wonder why Jonah's message was so convincing? Perhaps at heart, the citizens knew that their 'wickedness' would, at some point, have consequences. Perhaps they were ready to hear the news that they had to change.

God speaks to us still, in a variety of ways, urging us to care for our world, to be tireless advocates for justice, to support the weaker members of society and to work for peace. These are crucial aspects of our calling as Christ's followers. We need to make time in our busy, pressured lives, to stop, to listen and to hear.

Open our ears, Lord, that we may hear your voice among the distractions of our noisy world. Give us good discernment so that we may know what you ask of us and grant us the strength and wisdom to respond well. We ask this through Jesus Christ, our Lord. Amen.

AMANDA BLOOR

What have you done?

When God saw what they did, how they turned from their evil ways, God changed his mind about the calamity that he had said he would bring upon them, and he did not do it. But this was very displeasing to Jonah, and he became angry. He prayed to the Lord and said, 'O Lord! Is not this what I said while I was still in my own country? That is why I fled to Tarshish at the beginning, for I knew that you are a gracious God and merciful.'

This scene is almost comical, but it is tragic too, as we can easily recognise the human truths that lie behind it. Jonah thinks only of himself and the unfairness of the task that God gave him, rather than remembering the many lives that were at stake in Nineveh. Furious and embarrassed, his dignity in tatters, he rails at God. 'I knew that you'd do this! It's so unfair! I might as well be dead!'

I find myself having a sneaking sympathy for Jonah. He was told to do something difficult and potentially dangerous; it was made clear to him, via a storm and a whale, that there was no escape; and when he preached doom to Nineveh, he was made to look foolish because of God's mercy towards the repentant citizens there. The calamity he prophesied did not come to pass. Yet the difference that Jonah's actions made was incalculable. The whole of that 'great city,' its people, its animals, even its very stones, were saved. In God's eyes, that is success.

When we offer ourselves in service, we never know quite what God might ask of us and what the results could be. Far too often we might feel that we have failed because the things that we had expected do not come to pass, but we do not have the whole picture. God sees, God knows and God's plans are good.

Sometimes, Lord, I find myself unable to trust, caught up in my own fears and anxious about my own future. The things I have done can feel worthless. Give me strength to carry on, secure in the knowledge of your guidance and wisdom. Amen.

AMANDA BLOOR

Having compassion

God said to Jonah, 'Is it right for you to be angry about the bush?' And he said, 'Yes, angry enough to die.' Then the Lord said, 'You are concerned about the bush, for which you did not labour and which you did not grow; it came into being in a night and perished in a night. And should I not be concerned about Nineveh, that great city, in which there are more than a hundred and twenty thousand persons?'

I can picture a furious Jonah sitting in the heat of the sun under the bush that God has grown to give him shelter. In the distance, he can glimpse Nineveh; a reminder of God's irritating tendency towards mercy. When the next morning the bush withers away and the sun beats relentlessly on Jonah's head, he is even more angry. He resents God offering him shade, but he is livid when it is taken away.

The book of Jonah gives the reluctant prophet frequent opportunities to discover what it is that God considers important, to trust in God's guiding hand and to think of others instead of himself. It seems, however, that Jonah is unwilling to learn from his many experiences, but instead to repeat his mistakes. If we are being honest, we can probably recognise that same tendency in ourselves.

We might expect the book to come to a neat conclusion, where Jonah has learned to be more generous towards others and more trusting of God's purposes. Yet the story comes to a halt with the reminder that if the death of a bush caused Jonah pain, the fate of the people of a whole city matters deeply to God. We are not told if Jonah, this time, accepted the lesson. I hope he did, because that gives me hope that I too can learn from my errors and, in God's mercy, begin again.

All-seeing, all-knowing, all-merciful God, grant to us the same generosity of spirit towards others that you extend to us. You are our eternal creator, our defender in times of trouble. Forgive us our lack of compassion towards others and daily fill our hearts with your love. Amen.

AMANDA BLOOR

The God who dwells

The Bible takes the existence of God, that God is with us, for granted. The question it wrestles with is how God is with people and how people respond or relate to God.

Some scholars see John's gospel as the reflections of a small, fragile, fragmented Christian community, telling their story and understanding of who Jesus is and who they are. It offers responses to one of the first questions put to Jesus by those around him: 'Who are you?' In Jesus is a revelation of how God dwells in us.

We dwell in God. Jesus, and the stories and words round him, reveal how God is 'among us' and the ways in which people respond or relate to God. Jesus invites his followers to abide, to remain in him. The word 'abide/remain' from the Greek root *meno* occurs 34 times in John. It first occurs in 1:32–33 to refer to the Holy Spirit remaining on Jesus at his baptism.

'Dwell' could be said to be a summary of the gospel according to John in one word. If the word *meno* carries the idea of remaining, the Greek word *skeno* in 1:14 is translated as 'dwell and live'. The word appears twice in Revelation – in 21:3, where it refers to the home and dwelling of God, and 7:15, where we have an image of God who gives us our ultimate shelter and sanctuary. The same word occurs in Exodus 25:8, where we have God asking that the people 'make me a sanctuary so that I may dwell among them'.

It is a wonder of the gospel that the revelation of how God is with us is located in an area that was under Roman occupation and administration. It was an area of great diversity but also of conflict, danger and division. It is here we see Jesus engage with people and the powers that be, refusing to confine God to any one place, mountain or temple, calling people to fullness of life, unity and service amid struggle, sorrow and suffering. Here he gives people the 'power to become the children of God' (John 1:12) and assures them of strength.

Here, where people may well ask the age-old question 'Where are you, God?', or where does God dwell, is the revelation of how God dwells among us and how we can 'dwell' in God.

INDERJIT BHOGAL

And the Word became flesh

In the beginning was the Word, and the Word was with God, and the Word was God. He was in the beginning with God. All things came into being through him, and without him not one thing came into being. What has come into being in him was life, and the life was the light of all people... The true light, which enlightens everyone, was coming into the world... And the Word became flesh and lived among us.

The opening words 'in the beginning', recall the opening words of the Bible in Genesis 1:1, and root the story of Jesus and his first followers in the Hebrew scriptures and stories. Jesus is also given a home and an identity in God. The followers of Jesus whose reflections give us the gospel according to John see Jesus as the physical revelation and expression of the Word who was 'with God, and... was God' (v. 1).

The 'Word' is the cosmic, eternal, divine reality at the heart of all creation. The chief controversies and conflict in John (9:16; 10:19–20) are around the question of who is Jesus. The answer given in the opening words is that Jesus is God incarnate, he comes from God, he abides in God and brings life. This is stated consistently in the stories, controversies and discussions that follow, and emphatically stated in the words: 'I came that they may have life and have it abundantly' (10:10).

The source of all life, the true light that enlightens all people came 'into the world' and is revealed in Jesus. This is summed up in John in a profound declaration: 'And the Word became flesh and lived among us' (v. 14). The word translated 'lived' literally means 'pitched a tent, camped, made a sanctuary' among us. This is how holy and divine solidarity is described. God takes the initiative to come to dwell 'among us'.

In this understanding, in the face of Jesus Christ is seen the face of God; in his words are heard the word of God; his footprints are the footprints of God; his touch is the touch of God; his breath is the breath of God; his look is the gaze and grace of God; his actions are the actions of God.

Where in your experience do you see the footsteps of God, who is with you?

INDERJIT BHOGAL

The call to dwell in the divine

When Jesus turned and saw them following, he said to them, 'What are you looking for?' They said to him, 'Rabbi' (which translated means Teacher), 'where are you staying?' He said to them, 'Come and see.' They came and saw where he was staying, and they remained with him that day. It was about four o'clock in the afternoon.

In the reading today the word 'remain' appears twice, and it declares how God is with us and what our relationship with God is to be like. God remains with us, and we are called to remain with God.

The wider passage begins with John the Baptist pointing Jesus out to two of his own disciples, describing Jesus as the 'Lamb of God', who, he says, 'takes away the sin of the world' (1:29). The two disciples follow Jesus. Then we read that Jesus' first action is that he 'turned and saw' – a divine and fundamental act that initiates a relationship of intimacy and indwelling.

Taking away the sin of the world begins with turning and seeing the world as it is. This first action of Jesus begins to unpack what it means to say that 'the Word became flesh' (1:14). The holy one is present, God's gaze and attention is fixed on us, to take sin away.

Then the primordial, perennial question for followers of Jesus: what is it that you are looking for? The question could be stated as 'What kind of Jesus are you looking for?' or 'What are you looking for from Jesus?' Then the first question put to Jesus is: 'Where are you staying?', or where does God dwell? In the midst of all human experience and sin and wrestling with the meaning of existence arises the question: where is God?

Jesus' response, 'Come and see', is not an answer, more an invitation – into companionship. The disciples 'came and saw… and… remained with him'. They then went and 'brought' others to such discipleship.

God dwells with us. Discipleship begins with an invitation to 'remain', to dwell with God, and for Simon to become Cephas (Peter).

What questions would you have put to Jesus as one of his first disciples?

INDERJIT BHOGAL

Abundance and banquet

On the third day there was a wedding in Cana of Galilee, and the mother of Jesus was there. Jesus and his disciples had also been invited to the wedding. When the wine gave out, the mother of Jesus said to him, 'They have no wine'… 'Everyone serves the good wine first and then the inferior wine after the guests have become drunk. But you have kept the good wine until now.' Jesus did this, the first of his signs, in Cana of Galilee and revealed his glory, and his disciples believed in him.

The reading today begins with the words 'on the third day', which in John is the day that depicts life and transformation of life (2:20–22). The context here is a wedding feast, and Jesus is a guest, the life and soul of the party. 'The mother of Jesus' is present at this party, as she is in the pain and heartache of Jesus' crucifixion, watching and waiting by his side (John 19:25).

In Jesus' context, wedding feasts could last several days. It is not a surprise, in the words of the observant Mary, that 'they have no wine'. She calls upon Jesus and instructs the attendants to follow his directions. This is an essential requirement to what follows.

Jesus instructed them to 'fill' the jars which are there for ritual purposes with water. He then asked for some of this water to be taken to the 'chief steward'. When the chief steward tasted the water which had now become wine, he commended the bridegroom for the 'good wine'. He heaped praise on the bridegroom for reserving the best wine till the end of the celebration.

Abundance and banquet: this is a sign of the presence and desire of God. God dwelling with us first and foremost brings and draws out abounding goodness and service, qualities that reflect 'good wine'. This recalls God's own reflection upon the work of creation: 'It was very good' (Genesis 1:31). Creative and abounding goodness reflects the very nature of God.

Jesus had been 'invited' there, as had his disciples. The ministry of life is for Jesus and all his community.

Where and when have you experienced the abundant grace of God?

INDERJIT BHOGAL

God dwells in situations of struggle

When Jesus saw him lying there and knew he had been there a long time, he said to him, 'Do you want to be made well?' The ill man answered him, 'Sir, I have no one to put me into the pool when the water is stirred up, and while I am making my way someone else steps down ahead of me.' Jesus said to him, 'Stand up, take your mat and walk.'

The context of this story is a 'festival' and a celebration. Our reading homes in on a man who has been ill for 38 years. Jesus' gaze falls upon this man. Jesus 'knew' that the man 'had been there a long time' and seemed to be familiar with his story.

The pool mentioned, with five porticos, would catch the gaze of visitors. They could not have missed the many people with various ailments sitting and lying there, waiting for the water to be 'stirred up'. This stirring represents a sign of God's presence amid what may signify chaos. It recalls the words in Genesis 1:2: 'The earth was complete chaos, and darkness covered the face of the deep, while a wind from God swept over the face of the waters.' The Bible insists that God the creator dwells in the depths of tough realities, opening up new creation and life.

Jesus did not question the idea of healing in the stirred water. He only questioned what kept the man before him from achieving health, asking him, 'Do you want to be made well?' This is Jesus' second critical question in John. The man's reply avoids Jesus' question.

Jesus then spoke empowering words no one else appears to have uttered to the man before: 'Stand up, take your mat and walk.' The man is immediately 'made well', so took his mat and walked. Just as another celebration beckons at this restoration, a pause button is pressed. Controversy ensues with the words 'Now that day was a Sabbath' (John 5:9).

Having been declared 'the Saviour of the world' (John 4:42), Jesus enters a life of persecution from here on.

---

*What is your experience of being criticised
in the midst of doing good and creative work?*

INDERJIT BHOGAL

Abide in me for lasting nourishment

'Unless you eat the flesh of the Son of Man and drink his blood, you have no life in you. Those who eat my flesh and drink my blood have eternal life, and I will raise them up on the last day, for my flesh is true food, and my blood is true drink. Those who eat my flesh and drink my blood abide in me and I in them. Just as the living Father sent me and I live because of the Father, so whoever eats me will live because of me. This is the bread that came down from heaven... The one who eats this bread will live forever.'

The words of our reading are part of the discussion that follows the feeding of the multitude. The discussion includes reflections on what it is to be in relationship with Jesus. It digs deep into the history of God providing manna in the wilderness. Now Jesus offers the enduring 'bread of life' (John 6:35). Some people around him pray, 'Give us this bread always' (v. 34).

The focus is on divine food and nourishment that 'endures', in contrast to the food that 'perishes' (v. 27). These words point to the centrality of the sacrament of eating in Holy Communion. This is emphasised in the words 'Unless you eat the flesh of the Son of Man and drink his blood, you have no life in you.' To prevent readers from taking these words literally, John adds: 'It is the spirit that gives life; the flesh is useless' (v. 63).

These words evoke Eucharistic liturgy from early church experience. Only in John do we have reference to eating flesh in the context of the Eucharist. Conversations around the true meaning of Jesus' words about consuming flesh and blood began to emerge very early in church life.

This discussion notes that participating in the sacrament of Holy Communion was integral to participating in the life of Christ and in his community. This is how Jesus' community 'abide in me, and I in them'. Jesus invites his followers to openly enter this communion. For many of the people around Jesus this was a difficult and risky undertaking (v. 66).

Holy God, feed us with the bread of life always. Amen.

INDERJIT BHOGAL

Abide in me by my word

They did not understand that he was speaking to them about the Father. So Jesus said, 'When you have lifted up the Son of Man, then you will realise that I am he and that I do nothing on my own, but I speak these things as the Father instructed me. And the one who sent me is with me; he has not left me alone, for I always do what is pleasing to him.' As he was saying these things, many believed in him. Then Jesus said to the Jews who had believed in him, 'If you continue in my word, you are truly my disciples, and you will know the truth, and the truth will make you free.'

Jesus consistently asserts, as here, his closeness to God and that God is with him in all circumstances, not least when he is 'lifted up', words that allude to his crucifixion. These words are particularly addressed to those who are new followers of Jesus, who do not even 'understand that he was speaking to them about the Father'.

The presence of God is beyond doubt, but those who are less grounded in faith are offered another pathway to grow in faith. Jesus encourages them to be rooted in scripture. They are invited to dwell on the word: 'If you continue in my word, you are truly my disciples.' Scripture affirms God is with us, and one way to grow a closer relationship with God and Christ is to 'continue in my word'.

Jesus' earliest communities dwelt on his words. They met regularly to remember Jesus and to hear again and again the stories and words of Jesus. For these first and newer followers of Jesus, recalling and reflecting on his words made Jesus' presence real, spoke to them of 'the Father' and strengthened their discipleship. Jesus said that two aspects of discipleship can result from being rooted in his words: 'You will know the truth, and the truth will set you free.'

These are complex ideas for all disciples of Jesus, as can be seen from the ensuing conversations in the gospel according to John. The words of Jesus challenged and questioned their allegiances and ideologies, as well as their claims of truth that bound them and called them to freedom.

'Let the word of Christ dwell in you richly' (Colossians 3:16).

INDERJIT BHOGAL

The abiding good shepherd

'The thief comes only to steal and kill and destroy. I came that they may have life and have it abundantly. I am the good shepherd. The good shepherd lays down his life for the sheep. The hired hand, who is not the shepherd and does not own the sheep, sees the wolf coming and leaves the sheep and runs away… I am the good shepherd. I know my own, and my own know me… And I lay down my life for the sheep.'

Today's reading offers rich imagery and sharp contrasts. The good shepherd, who knows the sheep, who enters by the gate and stays with the sheep, is contrasted with the 'hired hand', who is the complete opposite. The good shepherd offers only life in all its fulness, not to 'steal and kill and destroy' it.

The previous occurrence of 'good' in John is in reference to the best quality wine (John 2:10). Now goodness is related to the character of reliable presence and pastoral care, which is also integral to abundant life.

John 10 twice records the words 'I am the gate' (vv. 7, 9) and 'I am the good shepherd' (vv. 11, 14). The gate provides a flow for sheep to 'come in and go out and find pasture' (v. 9). The shepherd guides and cares for the sheep. All good shepherds will ensure this constant process of coming into the fold and going out for the sake of edification and the fullness of life. This is a good model for all Christian life, mission and education.

Jesus is held up here as the gate and the good shepherd, a good leader who constantly opens pathways to good pasture, who does not run away from danger or disown his followers, and who seeks only the edification, not the exploitation, of anyone.

Abundant life is reflected in John in the overflowing wine at the wedding in Cana (John 2), the gushing water at the well (John 4), and the 'fragments' that were 'gathered up' at the feast on the hillside and the true food and drink that does not perish (John 6). It is the gift of God, the abiding good shepherd.

We are all called to a ministry of a good shepherd,
always directed at nurturing and enhancement of life.

INDERJIT BHOGAL

Death is not the end

Now a certain man was ill, Lazarus of Bethany, the village of Mary and her sister Martha… So the sisters sent a message to Jesus, 'Lord, he whom you love is ill.' But when Jesus heard it, he said, 'This illness does not lead to death; rather, it is for God's glory, so that the Son of God may be glorified through it.'

The remarkable story of the raising of Lazarus appears only in John. Lazarus, Mary and Martha of Bethany are introduced as ones whom Jesus loved. Jesus may well have known Lazarus had a serious illness and was close to death. Mary and Martha will have expected Jesus to come to them immediately. But Jesus 'stayed' where he was a further two days before coming to Bethany.

Jesus linked illness and death to God's glory and the glory of the Son of God through this. Jesus' disciples did not want him to go to the region of Bethany because of threats to his life (v. 8).

Jesus faces two requests. One calls him to Bethany, while Jesus' disciples plead with him to stay where he was. Jesus engages with the fears of his disciples. He calls Lazarus 'our friend' and uses the term 'asleep' to refer to death (v. 11). The disciples misunderstand and again caution him against going to Bethany, arguing that if Lazarus has fallen asleep, 'he will be all right' (v. 12). When Jesus eventually insists on going to Bethany, one of his disciples, Thomas, says to the others, 'Let us also go, that we may die with him' (v. 16).

Mary and Martha want Jesus in one place; his disciples want him in another place. Jesus had no means of fast travel to get to Bethany before Lazarus died. Jesus goes to Bethany in spite of danger to his own life.

In John (9:3; 11:4), the concept of 'glory' and God's work is connected to suffering. It is the gospel pattern, in the words we read in Luke 24:26: 'Was it not necessary that the Messiah should suffer… and then enter into his glory?' The story of Lazarus, and its insight into the abiding God, requires a long-term view. It does not end with the death of Lazarus, but the eternal glory of God.

Glory to you, Holy God, in all that life brings. Amen.

INDERJIT BHOGAL

Abiding fragrance

Mary took a pound of costly perfume made of pure nard, anointed Jesus' feet, and wiped them with her hair. The house was filled with the fragrance of the perfume. But Judas Iscariot, one of his disciples (the one who was about to betray him), said, 'Why was this perfume not sold for three hundred denarii and the money given to the poor?'

The last verse in John 11 is clear: Jesus' life is in danger. John 12 opens with a date. It is 'six days before the Passover' (v. 1), a reminder that Jesus is entering the last week before his crucifixion. Jesus returns to Bethany. He is at the table with Lazarus, the story continues, and Jesus finds strength in meeting and eating with his friends. It is a sacramental meal. Martha serves, but the focus turns to Mary, who anoints Jesus' feet with precious perfume.

Each of the four gospels records the story of a woman anointing Jesus, but only in John is the woman named. There is an outrageous intimacy in Mary wiping Jesus' feet with her hair. The whole house is filled with the fragrance of the perfume, none of those present could miss it. The aroma recalls the fragrance in Genesis 8:21, where we read that God commits to a new covenant with all humanity.

Some of those present might have been incensed by this outpouring of devotion. One expressed shock verbally and raised questions about the appropriateness of using expensive perfume. The money could have been used to care for those in need. The one raising this objection is named as Judas, who is described as a 'thief', a characteristic of bad shepherds noted in 10:1.

Jesus' response to this criticism is that the poor are always 'with you' (v. 8). His community is not to be known for their charitable distribution of money to the poor, laudable as that may be. Rather, are they a community 'with', alongside, the poor? That's where God is according to scripture. Jesus alluded to this when he quoted Psalm 82:6 (see John 10:34), where God is shown to judge all who put themselves in the position of 'gods' by whether they stand with those who are most excluded and give them 'justice'.

Bring us, Holy God, to community and solidarity
with those in poverty. Amen.

INDERJIT BHOGAL

Love one another

'"Where I am going, you cannot come." I give you a new commandment, that you love one another. Just as I have loved you, you also should love one another. By this everyone will know that you are my disciples, if you have love for one another.'

Jesus is clear that while his death is not the end of the story for him or his disciples, it is the pathway to glory. Jesus is 'going to God' (John 7:33; 13:3). His disciples do not fully grasp this message. He is clear that his earthly sojourn is 'little' and is followed by another journey. Jesus addresses his disciples as 'little children' who struggle to comprehend this.

Jesus instructs his disciples to focus their attention on those around them and to 'love one another'. Jesus has modelled this love in the foot-washing act of service and sharing of food. If his followers are wondering why they have to do this, Jesus explains that the purpose of such love, above all, is that others will 'know that you are my disciples'. This is to be the focus of Jesus' disciples among themselves, and this is what is attractive and appealing to others.

Peter responds to these words of Jesus with a question related to where Jesus is going rather than the challenges of immediate relationships. His question leads to an important discussion in the context of betrayals and denials by his best friends (vv. 36–38).

This discussion begins in today's reading, which stresses again the pattern of the gospel as revealed in Jesus. Death does not have the final word, and the path of glory is laid with pain and suffering. One of the earliest poems in church hymnody describes this pattern well (Philippians 2:5–11). This is the path for all who would follow the way of Jesus; it sets them free from death and brings them home to God, where they will 'follow afterward' (v. 36).

This lengthy discussion concludes with Jesus' words 'Let us be on our way' (14:31). Jesus is going to his crucifixion, the way to his 'glory'. Jesus' first followers lived with some uncertainties and found focus and strength in each other and Jesus' words to 'love one another'.

Holy God, give us wisdom to grow in our love for one another. Amen.

INDERJIT BHOGAL

You know the way

'And you know the way to the place where I am going.' Thomas said to him, 'Lord, we do not know where you are going. How can we know the way?' Jesus said to him, 'I am the way and the truth and the life. No one comes to the Father except through me. If you know me, you will know my Father also. From now on you do know him and have seen him.'

The opening words of our reading are a continuation of Jesus' response to anxieties expressed in Peter's question, 'Where are you going?' (John 13:36). Jesus speaks to the 'troubled' heart of his community. He wants his followers to believe and rest in God and in him.

Jesus speaks of God's house with 'many dwelling places' (v. 2), or resting places, and he says, 'You know the way to the place where I am going.' Jesus is addressing Peter, who would deny him, to assure him that, in spite of his denial, 'where I am, there you may be also' (v. 3).

However, Jesus' disciples do not grasp what he says. Thomas expresses their difficulty: 'Lord, we do not know where you are going. How can we know the way?' The reply is summed up in the words: 'I am the way and the truth and the life. No one comes to the Father except through me.' Jesus' followers wrestle with these words, which do not end the discussion initiated with Peter's question.

Philip follows these words with a request: 'Lord, show us the Father, and we will be satisfied' (v. 8). Jesus' reply takes us back to the declaration 'the Word became flesh and lived among us' (John 1:14). In John, Jesus is the revelation of God, the physical expression of the Father: 'Whoever has seen me has seen the Father' (v. 9).

In John, Jesus' community constantly misunderstood his words. There were disputes and divisions in people around him. The questions of Peter, Thomas and Philip that draw all the responses from Jesus and deepen the conversation take place in the context of table fellowship, the last supper. The supper that recalls the Passover meal and is a foretaste of the heavenly banquet that is to come, the destiny.

Thank you, Holy God, for the many resting places on our journey. Amen.

INDERJIT BHOGAL

Abide in me

'Abide in me as I abide in you. Just as the branch cannot bear fruit by itself unless it abides in the vine, neither can you unless you abide in me. I am the vine; you are the branches. Those who abide in me and I in them bear much fruit, because apart from me you can do nothing.'

Vines are an image that Jesus' followers would have been familiar with. Biblical prophets used vines to symbolise faithfulness and fruitlessness in people's relationship with God. To see Jesus as the 'true' vine is to speak of his closeness to God, the vine grower. 'Abide in me as I abide in you', he says, calling disciples to also model a relationship of mutual indwelling.

Jesus calls his disciples to 'abide with me', and then speaks of the resulting fruit that is characterised by a capacity to 'remain' or endure; it has a quality of permanence (v. 16). In this part of John's gospel there are at least seven different references to the invitation to remain in Christ.

The followers of Jesus are seen as the branches of the true vine. The source of their life and sustenance is their relationship with Jesus. Only branches that remain connected to Jesus will bear fruit and can be more fruitful through pruning. Branches that bear no fruit are 'removed'.

Part of the fruit of abiding in Christ and his word is that the wishes and desires of his disciples are attuned to his and fulfilled. This includes deepening their response to the commandment to 'love one another'. The deepest expression of love is revealed when they 'abide in my love' (v. 9). One expectation of this is, in the words of Jesus, that 'my joy may be in you, and that your joy may be complete' (v. 11).

Abide in Christ – this is a way of understanding, developing, expressing and sustaining mission, a way of being disciples of Christ, and a way to grow and be fruitful and experience the fullness of life and joy. Jesus' words 'Abide in me' are not about being cosseted in Christ; rather, they reveal the way of being followers of Christ at all times and in all places.

Holy God, abide with me and show me the way to abide in you. Amen.

INDERJIT BHOGAL

He will guide you

'I still have many things to say to you, but you cannot bear them now. When the Spirit of truth comes, he will guide you into all the truth, for he will not speak on his own but will speak whatever he hears, and he will declare to you the things that are to come. He will glorify me because he will take what is mine and declare it to you.'

There is a promise in the words of Jesus of the Holy Spirit of God, 'the Spirit of truth', who will continue his work of being a source of guidance and strength in a hostile world, who will 'be with you forever' and who 'abides with you' (John 14:16–17).

The evidence of the work of the Spirit, also called 'the Advocate' (14:16, 26; 16:7), besides being a presence, includes being a strength and convicting the world of being 'wrong' about understandings of sin, righteousness and judgement (16:8–11). This is a monumental agenda to understand and undertake. No wonder we hear Jesus is reluctant to add to this list, declaring 'you cannot bear' more now.

But it is the work of the Spirit to 'guide you into all the truth', to 'speak whatever he hears', to 'declare to you the things that are to come', and to 'glorify' Jesus. The Holy Spirit is the guide, to lead Jesus' community along the way. The guidance and declaration will emerge from hearing.

Jesus is inviting his community now to reflect more deeply on the clues to God who dwells with us. This requires them to tune into and engage with the work of the Holy Spirit – to develop skills to hear and discern together where God is leading us and to declare what God is saying. This includes coming to grips with where we are all 'wrong', as well as uncovering and announcing where we discern truth and things to come.

The Spirit will always hear what God is saying – 'take what is mine', as Jesus says – and will constantly 'guide' his followers forward, if they remain open to being 'wrong' and open to new insights into the truth of God, seeking ever and only to 'glorify' God and Christ.

Holy God, be our guide as we seek to discern all your truth. Amen.

INDERJIT BHOGAL

That they may become completely one

'I ask not only on behalf of these but also on behalf of those who believe in me through their word, that they may all be one... The glory that you have given me I have given them, so that they may be one, as we are one, I in them and you in me, that they may become completely one, so that the world may know that you have sent me and have loved them even as you have loved me.'

The prayer in John 17 is sandwiched between words Jesus addresses to his anxious and troubled disciples facing persecution, calling them to 'take courage' (16:33), and his own arrest (18:1). Jesus asks God to protect his community from hatred and persecution and to 'sanctify them' (v. 17).

Then Jesus prays for 'those who will believe in me through their word'. This is Jesus' prayer for succeeding generations of his followers; it is Jesus' prayer for us. This is not a prayer for good ecumenical relationships and unity. It is not a prayer that all may be the same. It is a prayer for unity within Jesus' first communities.

Jesus' prayer is about embracing and including newcomers, with all their differences, 'that they may all be one. As you, Father, are in me and I am in you, may they also be in us' (v. 21). The prayer goes beyond kindness and cohesion in relationships towards a togetherness reflected ultimately in God – 'One, as we are one.' Such union is good evangelism (v. 21) and brings glory to fruition, remembering that the true meaning of glory, in John, is not power but the upholding of the cross, and this deepens union with God towards its completeness (v. 22).

This is what brings the world to 'know' (v. 23) the true meaning of Christ's presence and love. Jesus concludes his prayer by addressing God as 'Righteous Father' (v. 25), or Just Father, a title for God not used anywhere else in the New Testament. This is the God who dwells with us, whom Jesus' community is to make known. The last sentence of Jesus' prayer is that the love of this God of justice 'with which you have loved me may be in them and I in them' (v. 26).

How do we reflect this righteous God,
who dwells with us and who fills us with love?

INDERJIT BHOGAL

Malachi

This week, as we move into the season of Advent, we are engaging with the book of the prophet Malachi. This book is the last of the Old Testament, and Malachi is the last of the three who prophesied after God's people returned from exile in Babylon, the other two being Haggai and Zechariah. Malachi means 'my messenger' or 'my angel'. He is sent to speak God's word to his generation, to remind them of the honour and respect due to God and to warn them of the consequences of not remaining faithful. It is a very short book – only four chapters – so you may like to read the whole book through before we begin.

As we read, we will see how the religious leaders of Malachi's day have become discouraged and careless and the effect this has on the people. We will be reminded of the importance of worship, of integrity and of remaining faithful in our relationship with God and others. We will be presented with the challenge of sacrificial giving. We will be encouraged to link Malachi, the last Hebrew prophet, with John the Baptist, the forerunner of Jesus, recognising our common heritage. We will think too about how Malachi's words speak into our relationship with Jesus today.

Advent is a good time for us to engage with this hard-hitting prophet. As we enter what is often a busy season running up to Christmas, it is helpful to take a long hard look at our relationship with God. What needs to be enhanced, developed or renewed in our faith? What has become lacklustre in our worship or our prayer? As God looks at our churches today, what does God see? What might God wish to say to us during this season as we prepare our hearts to welcome Jesus, the child of Bethlehem?

When I was a fairly new Christian I heard a series of talks on the book of Malachi at a Christian festival. Malachi's words had a profound effect on my faith then. Preparing these reflections, I have been reminded of the challenge and wisdom of his words. So, as we enter into Advent with the prophet Malachi, let us be open to what the Lord wishes to say to us today.

CATHERINE WILLIAMS

Honour and respect for God

A son honours his father and a servant his master. If then I am a father, where is the honour due me? And if I am a master, where is the respect due me? says the Lord of hosts to you, O priests, who despise my name. You say, 'How have we despised your name?' By offering polluted food on my altar... By thinking that the Lord's table may be despised.

'With great power comes great responsibility' is a saying popularised in the Marvel *Spider-Man* comics and films. It carries weight because we expect our leaders to have integrity, honesty and grace, alongside their charisma. Sadly, a fall from grace seems never far from those in the public eye, and the media revels in bringing to light scandals surrounding those we place in high positions. This is as true for our church leaders as it is for those who lead our communities and nation.

Malachi the messenger begins by addressing the holy leaders of the day, the priests. The word from God is very challenging. The priests have forgotten their responsibilities towards the Lord and the people. God asks why the religious leaders no longer honour or respect him. The sacrifices offered at the altar are rotten, the leftovers that no one wants. The priests seem unaware that the way they worship shows indifference, apathy and lack of reverence for God. This attitude is conveyed to the people, who look to their priests for guidance and example. Rather than reverence for God, they see disdain and boredom. The people are being led astray.

'Honour your father and your mother', says the fifth commandment (Exodus 20:12). Respect for family, for those we live among, is often easier than respect and honour for God, whom we cannot see. But the first commandment for all of us is 'Love the Lord your God with all your heart and with all your soul and with all your strength' (Mark 12:30). As we enter the Advent season, let us pray for our church leaders, that they and we will offer the honour and respect due to God.

Lord God, may everyone in our church community love you
with their whole heart. Amen.

CATHERINE WILLIAMS

Endless praise

For from the rising of the sun to its setting my name is great among the nations, and in every place incense is offered to my name and a pure offering, for my name is great among the nations, says the Lord of hosts. But you profane it when you say that the Lord's table is polluted and its food may be despised. 'What a weariness this is,' you say, and you sniff at it, says the Lord of hosts.

John Ellerton's much-loved hymn 'The day thou gavest, Lord, is ended' contains the verse: 'As over each continent and island, each dawn leads to another day, the voice of prayer is never silent, nor do the praises die away.'

It is a reminder that every second of every day someone, somewhere is offering prayer and praise to God. Through Malachi, the Lord reminds the people that God's name is revered across the world, far beyond the people of Israel. From the Psalms we learn that the whole of creation praises God, and Jesus told the Pharisees that if his followers were silenced, then the stones would cry out in praise of the Messiah (Luke 19:40).

Sadly God's people tell Malachi that they are weary of worship, and they turn their noses up at God. Worship has become a burden. The priests are careless and uninterested, and the people's response to God is shallow.

Most of us have the privilege of worshipping openly and freely, whenever and wherever we choose. Given that, why do we sometimes find ourselves weary of worship and doing something else rather than attending church? What makes us turn up our noses at God? Has it all perhaps become too safe and familiar? Are we taking our relationship with God for granted? Throughout the centuries of Christianity, there have been followers of Jesus who have taken great risks to praise God's name. Some were even martyred for their faith. Today too there are Christians who risk everything to worship the living God. As we journey through Advent, which is often a busy time of year in our modern world, let us commit to making the daily worship of God our priority.

Lord, from dawn to sunset, may I praise your holy name. Amen.

CATHERINE WILLIAMS

Family resemblance

I have sent this command to you, that my covenant with Levi may hold, says the Lord of hosts. My covenant with him was a covenant of life and well-being, which I gave him; this called for reverence, and he revered me and stood in awe of my name. True instruction was in his mouth, and no wrong was found on his lips. He walked with me in integrity and uprightness, and he turned many from iniquity.

What do you know about your ancestry? Seeking our roots and searching out family members is a popular pastime for many. Discovering common traits, trades and gifts in our families that have been passed down the generations can be fascinating. Do you have anyone famous in your family tree? Or infamous? Are you aware of a common thread that binds your people together?

Through the prophet Malachi, God reminds the priests of Israel of their common ancestor Levi, with whose clan God made a covenant of priesthood through Phinehas (Numbers 25:10–13). The clan of priests is called to revere God, teach truth and practise integrity. Levi was faithful to this. Unfortunately, Malachi finds that Levi's descendants are not: they have betrayed their calling and caused the people to stumble.

Beyond our immediate familial ties, we are all part of the one universal family, created, supported and loved by God. Within that family, Christians are also part of another family or clan. Through our baptism, we have been born afresh into the body of Christ, in which we all have a calling: a part to play. Our common ancestor is Jesus. We are part of his body, animated by the Holy Spirit to continue his work on earth. Through his death and resurrection, we have become the priesthood of all believers (see 1 Peter 2:9).

The words written about Levi in Malachi could also apply to Jesus, who walked with integrity, revealed truth and enabled many to turn to God. In what ways do you resemble your ancestor Jesus? How well do you relate to the other descendants of Jesus? How might you change or grow to enhance the family resemblance?

Lord Jesus, thank you for calling me into your family.
Help me grow more into your likeness. Amen.

CATHERINE WILLIAMS

Sibling rivalry

Have we not all one father? Has not one God created us? Why then are we faithless to one another, profaning the covenant of our ancestors? Judah has been faithless, and abomination has been committed in Israel and in Jerusalem, for Judah has profaned the sanctuary of the Lord, which he loves, and has married the daughter of a foreign god.

Sibling rivalry can be a problem in families. As a parent, I know my love reaches each of my children. They do not need to compete for it. But as a child, I fought with my siblings for our parents' attention. We were envious of each other. Bickering and jealousy can be exhausting. It is as though something in us stops us from recognising that our parents' unconditional love will stretch to each of us. Children need to learn to live well with others as they grow into their individuality.

Imagine this on a global scale. Unchecked rivalry between clans, tribes and nations leads to conflict and war, sometimes rumbling on for years down the generations, creating toxic communities and doing untold damage. Such violence comes from deep-seated insecurity, leading to the need to be more powerful and admired than others.

Through Malachi, God's attention turns from the priests to the people, reprimanding them for their inability to remain faithful to God and one another. The knock-on effect of becoming faithless and lax towards God can lead to damaged relationships and unhealthy behaviour towards others.

It is good to be reminded that we are all created equal, by the one God who parents us all. God's steadfast love is for everyone. We do not need to compete with one another for it. God cannot love any of us less – there is more than enough love to go around. We see this in the total love of Jesus, who sacrificed himself for us.

Why, then, do we sometimes struggle to remain faithful to God and one another? Be curious about any envy you feel towards another. What is fuelling that emotion in you? How might seeing others through God's eyes help you in your relationships?

Lord God, thank you for creating us all.
Teach me to see others with your eyes of love. Amen.

CATHERINE WILLIAMS

109

Preparing for the Lord

See, I am sending my messenger to prepare the way before me, and the Lord whom you seek will suddenly come to his temple... But who can endure the day of his coming, and who can stand when he appears? For he is like a refiner's fire and like washers' soap; he will sit as a refiner and purifier of silver, and he will purify the descendants of Levi and refine them like gold and silver, until they present offerings to the Lord in righteousness.

Advent is a season of preparation, when we make ready our hearts to receive Jesus, as the child of Bethlehem and as the one who comes to judge the world in the last days. We are good at preparing our homes for Christmas. Decorated trees, cards, presents and food may feature on our agendas and shopping lists. It is also important that we prepare our souls for the renewed presence of Christ among us. This requires space, prayer and a letting go of those things which keep our minds and hearts from seeking God.

Malachi is the last of the prophets in the Old Testament, and he points the way to the first of the prophets in the New Testament. Our passage today directly links to John the Baptist, and these verses, together with Isaiah 40:3, are quoted at the beginning of Mark's gospel (Mark 1:1–2). The messenger being sent will prepare the way for the Lord to come. John the Baptist fulfils that role for Jesus. He points to Jesus and prepares people by calling them to turn around and renew their relationship with the living God. This spiritual renewal cleanses, purifies and puts them back on track.

The imagery is stark. A refining fire is needed that will cleanse us of all impurities and make us shine like precious silver or gold. The soap referred to (older versions translate it as 'fullers' soap') is a caustic soap used to wash and soften wool so that it becomes pliable and good to wear next to the skin.

In these weeks before Christmas, both Malachi and John the Baptist encourage us to prepare for the Lord's coming. What might need softening in your heart? Where might you need some cleansing and refining to be ready to meet and greet Jesus?

Lord Jesus, soften my heart and cleanse my soul. Amen.

CATHERINE WILLIAMS

Grace-filled giving

Will anyone rob God? Yet you are robbing me! But you say, 'How are we robbing you?' In your tithes and offerings! You are cursed with a curse, for you are robbing me – the whole nation of you! Bring the full tithe into the storehouse… and thus put me to the test, says the Lord of hosts; see if I will not open the windows of heaven for you and pour down for you an overflowing blessing.

In today's hard-hitting passage, Malachi the messenger tells the people that they are robbing God by not giving the full tithe, the standard of giving expected of God's people in the law of Moses. Everything is given by God, who asks the people to return ten percent of it to help the community flourish. There are very few places in the Bible where God asks to be put to the test; this is one of them. God promises to pour overflowing blessings on those who give faithfully.

An important part of the refining and softening that we might need to do during this Advent season is to take a long, hard look at the way we give to God. This includes our time, skills and regular financial giving. While the Old Testament standard of giving was a ten percent tithe, in Jesus we move beyond this into a place of grace-filled sacrificial giving, recognising the gift of Jesus who gave his life for us. Tithing plus grace is the new standard for Christians.

This can be difficult to hear, yet those Christians who have learned to give sacrificially know first-hand the blessings of this spiritual discipline. Such giving is a joy and not the burden it might seem. The only way to experience this is to try it: put God to the test and see what happens. If all Christians were to embrace the joy of regular sacrificial giving our churches and communities would be transformed. It is important to grasp that everything we have comes from God and belongs to God. God gave everything for us in Jesus and now asks us to give back a small percentage for the good of all.

Lord God, fill my giving with your grace. Amen.

CATHERINE WILLIAMS

Leaping like calves

See, the day is coming, burning like an oven, when all the arrogant and all evildoers will be stubble; the day that comes shall burn them up, says the Lord of hosts, so that it will leave them neither root nor branch. But for you who revere my name the sun of righteousness shall rise, with healing in its wings. You shall go out leaping like calves from the stall.

Many of us will have seen newborn lambs and know how they frolic and bounce with energy and life, almost as if they have springs for legs. But have you seen newborn calves when they are let out of the barn for the first time? They too run and jump joyfully as they enter the fields and encounter grass and wide skies. Everything is new, fresh and to be explored.

In our final reading from Malachi, the people are warned that the day of the Lord is coming. It is the day when those who have not revered God's name and walked in God's ways will be no more. The imagery used is extreme and frightening. Those who have not remained faithful will be burnt up like the stubble left in the fields after the harvest.

The promise is very different for those who have honoured God. They will walk in the healing sunshine and leap with the energy of newborn liberated calves. The day of the Lord will be a joyous day of freedom for God's people.

As we continue through Advent, taking time to renew our walk with the living God, so we look towards the day of the Lord. This day comes with the birth of a child at Bethlehem and will come again when Jesus returns. Through the gift of Jesus, we are assured of a secure future in God. The popular carol 'Hark! The herald angels sing' by Charles Wesley and George Whitefield draws on the words of Malachi: 'Hail the heaven born Prince of Peace! Hail the Sun of Righteousness! Light and life to all he brings, risen with healing in his wings.'

When we sing those words at Christmas, let us recall the freedom and joy promised to all people in Jesus.

'Hark! The herald angels sing, "Glory to the newborn king."' Amen.

CATHERINE WILLIAMS

Matthew's Advent

 I love the season of Advent. It is so good I think, to start off the Christian year by looking ahead to the amazing time when Jesus will come again in glory. I like to celebrate Advent in this way for the full four weeks! On the other hand, I am disappointed when this vital aspect of Advent gets overshadowed, or even taken over entirely, by thoughts of Christmas. I could cite the majority of Advent calendars as evidence.

But we have before us, over the next two weeks, the longest statement made by Jesus on this subject of his eventual return in glory – and he does not pull any punches about the hard times that come first – or when it comes to the part about judging 'the living and the dead'.

Within the two chapters which this long dissertation occupies, we can find a number of parables, some clear prophetic words and a series of warnings. In all these, Jesus is preparing his current and future followers to be ready, both for his future advent and for what may happen in the times immediately before that amazing event. We are living in that interim period. These parables, prophecies and warnings are for each of us who follow Jesus, just as they were for each of his disciples then and for every disciple since.

I have to confess, I sometimes skips these chapters, favouring the other gospel accounts which don't mention Jesus' graphic but very uncomfortable prophecy of the throne of judgement, which form some of our closing readings. Perhaps we all feel a measure of guilt when we hear or read those words. However, with belief in the everlasting forgiveness that we have through the death and resurrection of our Lord Jesus Christ, we can look forward to that invitation from the great judge: 'Come and possess the kingdom which has been prepared for you ever since the creation of the world' (Matthew 25:34, GNT). This is the good news of the Advent season.

There will be time enough to look backwards to what happened at Christmas. Now is the time to be looking forward – to Advent!

Editor's note: Paul died not long after completing these reflections for us, and some of his comments read poignantly now he is with the Lord. We pray for those who grieve his loss and rejoice with him in resurrection life. Amen.

PAUL GRAVELLE

Demolition!

Jesus left and was going away from the Temple when his disciples came to him to call his attention to its buildings. 'Yes,' he said, 'you may well look at all these. I tell you this: not a single stone here will be left in its place; every one of them will be thrown down.'

In Matthew 23, Jesus has been weeping – yes, really weeping by the sound of it – over the future that he saw in store for Jerusalem. Now he is offering his disciples a prophetic warning that all the magnificent architecture they were admiring was to be utterly destroyed.

This temple, rebuilt after the Jewish exile in Babylon, was certainly something to be admired. Some of its stones were green-white in colour and over 12 metres long. The front of the building was sheathed in gold plate! Its later destruction by the Romans was to be the 9/11 of its day. Yes – even 9/11 seems a long time ago for us now. There have been many catastrophic events since then involving the destruction of buildings and loss of life. There may well be many more yet and – if I am sounding like a prophet of doom – so, in his day, was Jesus.

The warnings and prophecies in these chapters were certainly given for his immediate followers, those of his day. But Matthew has recorded them for those who succeeded him – people like us who are experiencing the things that Jesus prophesied would happen.

As you read on through the next verses and reflections, can you honestly say that we are not experiencing some of the things which Jesus prophesied? If we are experiencing them, we must recognise how important it is to take action in response to all the warnings that he gives us. These warnings are not only about being watchful and ready; they also make it clear that we are expected to be productive and 'fruitful'. Watch out for these warnings in the parables Jesus teaches!

Lord Jesus, please keep me from getting caught up in preparing to celebrate Christmas. I want to give proper attention to your forthcoming Advent. Please let these readings and reflections guide and help me in this. Amen.

PAUL GRAVELLE

Such things must happen

Many men… will come and say, 'I am the Messiah!' and they will fool many people. You are going to hear the noise of battles close by and the news of battles far away; but do not be troubled. Such things must happen, but they do not mean the end has come. Countries will fight each other… There will be famines and earthquakes everywhere. All these things are like the first pains of childbirth.

All through history since the first century, I suppose, people have been hearing these words of Jesus and been saying to each other, 'Ah, so it won't be very long now!' But, here we are. The wars, famines and earthquakes are still going on. There are probably a few pseudo-Messiahs around. We can even add floods, fires and further problems to the list. But we are still waiting for that second Advent which Jesus promised.

As we read on through the next few days, we will see that Jesus has quite a bit more to say on the subject. But let us not skip over this part too quickly. It would be very easy to take the attitude that because these things have always been happening, that 'the first pains of childbirth' will go on going on and that all will be well, unless something changes.

Jesus does not choose his metaphor of childbirth lightly. A birthing is imminent! We may think the labour pains unnecessarily prolonged – I remember well how my wife was in labour for four long days with our first child (who is now a pensioner) – but it is a prophetic promise of Jesus, our God, that he will most certainly come again to put right the sorry mess we have made in his world.

We are seeing many wars, famines, earthquakes and also floods and wildfires. There may be a lot more still to come. Many who follow Jesus Christ are going through these horrors and working through their aftermaths at this very minute.

Lord Jesus, we remember before you all our brothers and sisters who are experiencing the loss of loved ones, property and livelihood through warfare, persecution and natural disasters. In your mercy, comfort and restore them, we pray. Amen.

PAUL GRAVELLE

Whoever holds out to the end

Then you will be arrested and handed over to be punished and be put to death. Everyone will hate you because of me. Many will give up their faith at that time; they will betray one another and hate one another. Then many false prophets will appear and fool many people. Such will be the spread of evil that many people's love will grow cold. But whoever holds out to the end will be saved. And this Good News about the Kingdom will be preached through all the world for a witness to all people; and then the end will come.

In Matthew 24—25, more than at any other place in the gospels, we see Jesus in his role of prophet. Even the parables which the chapters contain are highly prophetic in nature. Jesus is acting very much like the Old Testament prophets before him, warning his friends and all who will come after him down through the ages about what to expect if they dare to believe.

All through history, these prophecies have proved to be true. When I was writing, legislation was being considered here in New Zealand in an effort to counter 'hate speech', indicating that this is a growing contemporary concern.

False prophets? You may say that we have enough of those already without naming any names. They are here in New Zealand, just like everywhere else. I came very close to being deceived by one myself, when I was still living in the UK.

Because you are reading this, I am assuming you have not grown cold! Yet the spread of evil never slows. It spreads through schools, through homes, through workplaces, through sports clubs – yes, even churches and home groups. Enough bad news? The good news is that whoever holds out to the end will be saved!

What about that final statement? Surely the good news has now reached to the remotest corner of Planet Earth, hasn't it? Should not the end be imminent?

'Our Father in heaven, hallowed be your name, your kingdom come, your will be done, on earth as it is in heaven' (Matthew 6:9–10, NIV). Your coming we await. Amen! Come, Lord Jesus.

PAUL GRAVELLE

False prophets

Then, if anyone says to you, 'Look, here is the Messiah!' or 'There he is!' – do not believe it. For false Messiahs and false prophets will appear; they will perform great miracles and wonders in order to deceive even God's chosen people, if possible. Listen! I have told you this ahead of time. Or, if people should tell you, 'Look, he is out in the desert!' – don't go there; or if they say, 'Look, he is hiding here!' – don't believe it. For the Son of Man will come like the lightning which flashes across the whole sky from the east to the west. Wherever there is a dead body, the vultures will gather.

False prophets! We have seen a few of them, for sure, some greater than others – and there will, no doubt, be more. The verses preceding today's passage refer to an event which had already taken place – the statue of Zeus set up in the temple of Jerusalem by Antiochus Epiphanes in 168BC. Now, Jesus gives us a heads-up about false Messiahs and prophets still to come.

It should go without saying that if we hear some new teaching, we should at once check it out with scripture. More than that, these spurious messiahs and prophets, says Jesus, will perform miracles and wonders to deceive even God's chosen people, if possible. So Jesus also provides us with a litmus test: 'For the Son of Man will come like the lightning.' This saying would have been much harder to interpret for those who lived in the days before television and mobile phones, but what Jesus promises here is perfectly plain to us now.

We will be hearing a lot more about being ready for Jesus to return. These are the first hints. The eminent theologian Tom Wright is always pointing the church to what he sees as its principal task – working towards drawing heaven closer to earth and thus preparing for that great future event.

Lord, Holy Spirit, I ask you for your gift of discernment,
so that I may recognise and challenge any false prophet seeking
to deceive your chosen ones. Amen.

PAUL GRAVELLE

The coming!

Soon after the trouble of those days, the sun will grow dark, the moon will no longer shine, the stars will fall from heaven, and the powers in space will be driven from their courses. Then the sign of the Son of Man will appear in the sky; and all the peoples of earth will weep as they see the Son of Man coming on the clouds of heaven with power and great glory. The great trumpet will sound, and he will send out his angels to the four corners of the earth, and they will gather his chosen people from one end of the world to the other.

Here, from Jesus' own lips, comes the prophetic proclamation of his second Advent in all its majesty and glory. I have on my desk a *Christus Victor* 'icon' depicting Christ, the cross behind him, robed and crowned in majesty, arms outstretched to gather his people. This is what some early Christians expected as the 'sign of the Son of Man'.

It would take an astrophysicist to comment adequately on the first sentence of this dramatic prophecy, but it clearly sets the scene for what is to follow – the return of the Son of Man, crowned with glory and honour, to judge the living and the dead.

Little wonder that the prophecy sees the 'peoples of earth' weeping in fear as they recognise their failure to believe while there was still time. Then comes the great trumpet call to summon the church – and I would like to offer a thought which I have found helpful as I move beyond four score and ten. The first creation story, in Genesis 1, tells us that God created time for us to live in. When we die, we pass from time into eternity, where there is no time! This being so, when I die, I will find myself instantly responding to that trumpet call, with all the church who are alive at the time. It was Jesus' promise to the dying thief: 'Today you will be in Paradise with me' (Luke 23:43). I believe that it will hold good for me. Earth will be paradise when Jesus is king!

God of hope, when Christ your Son appears,
may he find us active in his service and ready. Amen.

PAUL GRAVELLE

They did not realise

No one knows, however, when that day and hour will come – neither the angels in heaven nor the Son; the Father alone knows. The coming of the Son of Man be like what happened in the time of Noah. In the days before the flood people ate and drank, men and women married, up to the very day Noah went into the boat; yet they did not realise what was happening until the flood came and swept them all away. That is how it will be when the Son of Man comes.

Jesus gives two examples of what it will be like when he comes again. We will read about the second tomorrow, but in this first one, he emphasises the fact that there will be no universal warning. That trumpet will sound not as an early warning, but as a fanfare announcing that the king has already arrived!

I can remember, during the Blitz, that bombs would sometimes begin falling even before the air-raid warnings sounded. Day after day we are hearing fresh news of floods, earthquakes or other natural disasters overtaking various communities without warning. The final verse in this series of readings is about always being ready (Matthew 24:44).

Yet we must be ready in another way. I am thinking about being ready to share the good news with our neighbour or at least to say something which will start them thinking. One of the most important – and probably the most difficult – tasks which we have before us until our Lord returns is that of warning unsuspecting people of the danger they are in if they stay outside the safety barrier provided by belief in the risen Jesus.

I try not to imagine what it would be like hearing someone I know call out, 'Why didn't you tell me?', when the time to tell has passed and it is too late! We should all be haunted by that thought.

Lord, it is so hard to speak about you to others. Please give me the opportunity, the right words and above all the determination to share peaceable words with someone I meet today so that they will be ready when you come. Amen.

PAUL GRAVELLE

One taken, one left

That is how it will be when the Son of Man comes. At that time two men will be working in a field: one will be taken away, the other will be left behind. Two women will be at a mill grinding meal: one will be taken away, the other will be left behind.

Jesus underlines the drama of his future coming. Here he shows another reason why 'all the peoples of the earth' will be weeping. It is because they realise that they have missed out on the opportunity of becoming part of God's 'chosen people'.

While Jesus is prophesying into the future, he does not leave any middle ground. When he returns, he says, some will be taken and the others left. The same option for the future faces everyone then and now.

There has been a line of fiction on this topic which seems to have got things a little out of order here, but the need to become one of God's people remains, and it is as urgent as ever. Jesus did not hesitate to put the frighteners on his hearers then. Have we perhaps become too gentle in our calls to the unfaithful?

Here in Aotearoa, New Zealand, we are building on higher ground to avoid floodwaters and strengthening older buildings to avoid earthquake damage. There is a universal need for God's people everywhere to help their neighbours to understand what it would mean to be 'left behind' when the end comes. And I know that I must include myself in this injunction.

Concern for those who remain blind to their danger in this way is always heightened when it comes to members of our own family. We have probably overdone our warnings. They know the truth. Any more from us will only do harm. We should pray that someone else will say exactly the right thing to them. So, let us pray.

Lord Jesus Christ, we offer you all the truths from your word we have spoken to _____. We ask now that you will bring someone into their orbit who will cause them to respond to you and not to be left behind when you come again in your glory. Amen.

PAUL GRAVELLE

Parable 1: the fig tree

Let the fig tree teach you a lesson. When its branches become green and tender and it starts putting out leaves, you know that summer is near. In the same way, when you see all these things, you will know that the time is near, ready to begin. Remember that all these things will happen before the people now living have all died. Heaven and earth will pass away, but my words will never pass away.

Jesus uses six parables in this long discourse about his future return and the events leading up to it. This one comes first, but it is easy to get a bit confused. Is Jesus applying the fig tree parable to his own second coming in the events we were reflecting upon last Sunday or to the impending destruction of Jerusalem by the Romans? I think we can safely say he is applying it to both.

His words were true for AD70, when the bulldozing Romans came. His words are equally true for when the sign of the Son of Man appears and that vibrant trumpet sounds. His words will never pass away!

The fig tree, alongside the olive, was the most familiar of trees in the environment where Jesus lived. Everyone was used to looking to the fig tree for signs of a coming spring and summer. Even here, in North Island, Aotearoa, where evergreen varieties predominate, we look for signs of summer from the deciduous Jacaranda.

From time to time down through the ages, history has seen false prophets who misread the signs of their times and proclaim that the Lord's coming is imminent. What Jesus is saying through this parable applies both to AD70 and AD2025. Remember, signs of spring do not mean that summer has already arrived, only that 'the time is ready to begin'.

If we expand the parable a little, every one of God's people has urgent duties to perform in his service besides 'checking on the fig tree'!

Lord, we believe that your words will never pass away. Help us, we pray, both to recognise the first buds on any branch of your proverbial fig tree and to nurture the other plants in your garden. Amen.

PAUL GRAVELLE

Parable 2: the two servants

Who, then, is a faithful and wise servant? It is the one that his master has placed in charge of the other servants to give them their food at the proper time. How happy that servant is if his master finds him doing this when he comes home! Indeed, I tell you, the master will put that servant in charge of all his property. But if he is a bad servant, he will tell himself that his master will not come back for a long time, and he will begin to beat his fellow servants and to eat and drink with drunkards. Then that servant's master will come back one day when the servant does not expect him… The master will cut him in pieces and make him share the fate of the hypocrites.

Parable number two has an uncompromisingly unpleasant ending. This is, of course, a sharp warning to those of us in any kind of leadership position. But it is not directed at us alone: each one of us is a servant of the king and, although we do not know its time, we have his promise that he is absolutely, definitely coming back! When he does, he will naturally expect to know what we have been doing.

The bad servant in the story convinces himself that his master will not be back for a long time. Very risky! Or perhaps you think that this is all a bit over the top and that, once we believe, are baptised, saved or however we like to put it, it does not matter how we treat our fellow servants? Jesus clearly puts so much importance on this that he has the master punishing the bad servant almost to the point of death at the end of the story.

In what fresh way might you give your fellow servants what they need? Ask the Lord about it or think of something they have not experienced before. Why not surprise them?

Loving God, I know you will come back, because that is what you have promised. While I wait, I am your servant. Please show me new ways in which I may bless my fellow servants who are waiting with me. Even so, come, Lord Jesus. Amen.

PAUL GRAVELLE

Parable 3: the ten young women

At that time the Kingdom of heaven will be like this. Once there were ten young women who took their oil lamps and went out to meet the bridegroom. Five of them were foolish, and the other five were wise. The foolish ones took their lamps but did not take any extra oil with them, while the wise ones took containers full of oil for their lamps. The bridegroom was late in coming, so they began to nod and fall asleep. It was already midnight when the cry rang out, 'Here is the bridegroom! Come and meet him!'

Rather than go over the cultural background of Jewish weddings in those days, here are a few lines from a contemporary version I wrote some years ago for a Salvation Army youth leader to use – putting this parable in the context of a pop concert.

You five are out of Coke! You must be crazy – you can't mean it! You can't have some of ours, you should have been awake – foreseen it! You see the stall out there – they've got the stuff; I've seen it. I did my best, I warned of this and didn't I remind us to be prepared? Once we're inside, they'll never ever find us. Quick, move along! Oh! Too late now; they've closed the gate behind us!

We live in an era where there is a wealth of misunderstanding about what Christianity is all about. In my country, where secular education has been the rule for generations and many older people spent their childhood days in distant rural areas, far from a church, Christianity for the majority is a kind of club which meets on Sundays to sing hymns and drink cups of tea. There is, as yet, no oil in their lamps.

If you think about it, things are mostly no better where you are. There is no shortage of the oil of the Holy Spirit, but is there enough of that oil in your church? And how is it going to reach those people out there who have no oil in their lamps at all?

Lord, give me oil in my lamp,
enough to share with those whose lamps are dim. Amen.

PAUL GRAVELLE

Parable 4: the three servants

At that time the Kingdom of heaven will be like this. Once there was a man who was about to leave home on a trip; he called his servants and put them in charge of his property. He gave to each one according to his ability: to one he gave five thousand gold coins, to another he gave two thousand, and to another he gave one thousand. Then he left on his trip. The servant who had received five thousand coins went at once and invested his money and earned another five thousand. In the same way the servant who had received two thousand coins earned another two thousand. But the servant who had received one thousand coins went off, dug a hole in the ground, and hid his master's money.

This, of course, is the parable of the talents, from which we have come to think of a talent as something like piano-playing or metalwork. While this is apt, and we can see that some have more of this kind of talent than others, it is important to recognise opportunities as another form of talent – and we are all given many of them.

This is where we see the importance of recognising the situation into which the one-thousand-coin servant got himself in the parable. Unlike the other two, he – or she – failed entirely to use any of the opportunities that presented themselves. After all, interest alone is unlikely to have doubled the money of the other two servants. They had to have grabbed some other opportunities to have achieved that kind of success.

Before we got into thinking about thousands of coins, I often heard the 'talents' in this parable referring to new believers, won for or helped towards the kingdom, where there is eternal life. If you read on to the end of this parable at v. 30, while the one-thousand-coin servant receives drastic, remedial treatment, both the others receive a beautiful, 'Well done, good and faithful servant!' (v. 23). Let us pray that we may deserve that too!

Lord Jesus Christ, forgive me for all the opportunities
I have allowed to slip by. Please give me new opportunities to serve you
and help me recognise them in time. Amen.

PAUL GRAVELLE

Parable 5a: come, possess the kingdom!

When the Son of Man comes as King… he will sit on his royal throne, and the people of all nations will be gathered before him. Then he will divide them into two groups… the righteous people at his right and the others at his left. Then the King will say to the people on his right, 'Come, you that are blessed by my Father! Come and possess the kingdom which has been prepared for you… I was hungry and you fed me…' The righteous will then answer him, 'When, Lord, did we ever see you hungry…?' The King will reply, 'I tell you, whenever you did this for one of the least important of these followers of mine, you did it for me!'

While some might want to use this passage as an argument in favour of 'salvation by works', the response which the righteous people give shows that they had not been thinking that way.

This is a prophetic statement by Jesus which carries on directly from the one he gives just before the four parables. To get the full effect, you could turn back and re-read the passage for Thursday 11 December if you like.

Jesus as king recognises what the righteous ones have done to prepare the way for him. He invites them into the renewed kingdom of earth, now the fulfilment of the Old Testament prophets. With the king on the throne, the victory of the cross becomes effective across the breadth of planet earth.

We are not destined to inherit the kingdom of heaven; that is God's space. Our inheritance is this familiar planet of ours, renewed under the king of kings. We, our loved ones and all God's people who have moved into eternity before us, will respond to the trumpet call together.

This is where Advent reflections should end. But there is one scene that must still be played out, one warning we must heed before we start the celebration of Christmas.

Christus Victor, coming on the clouds, we worship you in anticipation of the glorious reign which you have promised to take up on our planet.
We rejoice over your promise to renew creation and release it from the powers of evil. Even so, come Lord Jesus. Amen.

PAUL GRAVELLE

Parable 5b: whenever you refused to help

Then he will say to those on his left, 'Away from me, you that are under God's curse! Away to the eternal fire which has been prepared for the Devil and his angels! I was hungry but you would not feed me…' Then they will answer him, 'When, Lord, did we ever see you hungry… and we would not help you?' The King will reply, 'I tell you, whenever you refused to help one of these least important ones, you refused to help me.' These, then, will be sent off to eternal punishment, but the righteous will go to eternal life.

Some would see this whole judgement scene as another parable, set in the context of the judicial system current in Jesus' time. Others would take a more literal view of Jesus' words. You must evaluate things for yourself, but we should note that Jesus' style in this whole section is unlike his usual pattern for parables and much closer to his prophetic language. Taken as a whole, scripture never avoids the matter of punishment for unrepented wickedness, and there is a large crowd at the King's left!

There are two things we should not miss in this whole picture of the last judgement. One is the apparent unawareness of the first group that they were doing anything for the King when they offered help to the needy. Second is the awareness of the King's existence which the second group clearly had, even while they were ignoring the needs of the poor.

I have often felt that, at the final judgement, we could find ourselves alongside people who have never attended church. There are some strange ideas around about Jesus' promised second coming, even among Christians. We have taken time over the past fortnight to see what Jesus himself says on the subject. He has not told us everything; he still leaves us room to talk further. For this purpose, you will find some suggested questions for discussion which I hope you will use, perhaps when the Christmas rush is over (see p. 146). Meanwhile, have a very blessed Christmas feast!

Lord God, we know that conditions must be fulfilled before your Son returns to us. May we fail in nothing that is required of us before that great and glorious day arrives. May we follow your ways of truth, beauty and justice until your kingdom comes. Amen.

PAUL GRAVELLE

Parable 6: as a thief in the night

Watch out, then, because you do not know what day your Lord will come. If the owner of the house knew the time when the thief would come, you can be sure that he would stay awake and not let the thief break into his house. So then, you must always be ready, because the Son of Man will come at an hour when you are not expecting him.

Do you think this is one of Jesus' little jokes – comparing himself to a thief? I think we might sometimes miss his sense of humour. This passage actually comes directly after the reading we shared on Saturday 13 December, but it is a good one with which to conclude Advent. It is all about being ready – being aware that Jesus expects us to be actively preparing for his second coming.

The theologian Tom Wright speaks and writes a lot about this. He uses this image of two overlapping circles, a Venn diagram representing the way in which heaven has begun to merge with earth ever since the resurrection. The merging will become complete at Jesus' second coming, but we, the church, are tasked with preparing the way for this to happen – not just sitting and waiting for it. We must always be ready.

Wright writes about working in areas such as truth, beauty and justice as ways to achieve God's purposes in this direction. I have stressed the need to recognise and action every opportunity that we can as we prepare for the sounding of that glorious trumpet which Jesus talks about.

Do you wonder how it will really happen? Jesus has said it will, and he has given us these tantalising hints as to how. We are called to be ready and waiting, but that also involves actively preparing for it all. And the most important action is prayer; 'Your kingdom come on earth as in heaven!'

PAUL GRAVELLE

Luke's Christmas

 Luke begins his gospel by telling us there were many accounts of the life of Jesus doing the rounds in the early church. We know Luke himself was a doctor. His 'orderly' (1:3, NIV) writing reflects the careful eye for detail you expect from one whose work requires a close observation of things. This means that we may trust what he writes. But if, on his own admission, the market was already flooded with gospel versions, why has he added yet another?

It seems he was writing to a man called Theophilus. We know no more about him except that he was a Gentile, clearly already a serious seeker, and probably quite a significant and influential presence in the early church and surrounding community. Luke addresses him with great courtesy and respect and has gone to enormous lengths to introduce him to Jesus: 'I myself have carefully investigated everything from the beginning... so that you may know the certainty of the things you have been taught' (1:3–4, NIV). This means that one of the gospel records actually began life as a private letter. Clearly, Theophilus shared it more widely, and it eventually became one of the four main accounts in the scriptures of the worldwide Christian church.

I have had to be selective in choosing these daily extracts from Luke's Christmas narrative. The Christmas story we tell in our churches is often a merger of details from the various gospel accounts, with some added dramatic imagination of our own! In fact, each gospel has its own way of telling the story of Jesus. I have tried to ensure that the features in the story that Luke particularly wants his readers to notice are found here.

For example, he gives women respectful prominence in his account – especially Mary. He stresses how the gospel is good news for the poor and the marginalised. They are given special welcome and inclusion – like the shepherds. The themes of joy, worship and prayer are woven through his whole account – as expressed here by the angels, Zechariah and Elizabeth. Above all this is the story of God's saving life and love breaking into the world through the coming of Jesus – as proclaimed through the prophetic faith of Simeon and Anna in the temple.

As Luke's Christmas unfolds, may we too 'know the truth' (v. 4, GNT) of what we read.

DAVID RUNCORN

Zechariah and Elizabeth

There was a priest named Zechariah... His wife was... Elizabeth. Both of them were righteous before God... But they had no children... and both were getting on in years. Once... he was chosen by lot... to enter the sanctuary of the Lord to offer incense... Then there appeared to him an angel of the Lord... and fear overwhelmed him. But the angel said to him, 'Do not be afraid... Your wife Elizabeth will bear you a son, and you will name him John'... Elizabeth conceived, and for five months she remained in seclusion.

The first people we meet in Luke's gospel are a devout couple called Zechariah and Elizabeth. They are childless and ageing. To be childless can be an abiding pain for a couple to endure, especially so in a culture where bearing children defines a woman's worth. Luke makes clear this is not a sign of God's judgement. But at this point, in human terms, the story can go no further.

In the Bible, barrenness, like virginity, is a symbol of something humanly impossible. A few verses later, Gabriel will appear to an unmarried virgin girl called Mary. So, this is beginning with people who, by any normal measures, are either too late or too soon for what the story requires. What God is doing is outside human expectation, capability and power. And with God nothing is impossible.

Zechariah is on duty in the holiest part of the temple at the time of the evening offering. Luke tells us all the people outside the sanctuary are gathered. Here is faithful Israel praying before their God. When Gabriel appears with the message that he will have a son and that Israel will have a great prophet, Zechariah, not unreasonably, struggles to believe this. Rather abruptly, the angel makes him deaf and mute!

Elizabeth conceives and she too goes into seclusion – though by choice. Perhaps she is showing a wisdom Zechariah needs help to learn. Both go into silence as the unexpected gift of new life stirs in her womb, in their marriage and ministry. Not everything God does or reveals is for talking about immediately. We need time to let it grow until it is ready to come to birth.

I pray for those who have prayed and hoped for a long time.
May their prayers be answered. Amen.

DAVID RUNCORN
The Fourth Sunday of Advent   129

The angel Gabriel

The angel Gabriel was sent by God… to a virgin engaged to a man whose name was Joseph, of the house of David… And he came to her and said, 'Greetings, favoured one! The Lord is with you… Do not be afraid, Mary… you will conceive in your womb and bear a son, and you will name him Jesus… Mary said to the angel, 'How can this be, since I am a virgin?' The angel said to her… 'The power of the Most High will overshadow you'… Mary said, 'Here am I… let it be with me according to your word.'

Do angels ever feel bewildered by their assignments? Angel means 'messenger'. Like civil servants, they do not have opinions. So, we do not know what Gabriel felt like appearing to the astonished, ageing Zechariah, to tell him he and Elizabeth are going to have a child. Here he is again, with the same message, but standing in front of a young, unmarried village girl called Mary. Did he double check if he had got the right address? Did he stop to wonder how this teenage girl would even survive the fallout from all this?

As so often in the Christmas story, the first message is 'Do not be afraid'. There is no one here who is not initially afraid and anxious. This is all beyond human understanding and expectation, but the message comes with the firm reassurance that this is God at work. Despite all appearances, he can be trusted. God knows what he is about.

Mary's question to the angel is very practical. How can this be possible at all? The answer is hidden in the overshadowing love of God. Notice how God invites her 'yes'. Divine love is not coercive. Mary makes her astonishing submission of trust and acceptance.

How honoured we are to be eavesdropping on a moment of such holy gift and intimacy. There, at the beginning of it all, Mary models what trusting faith is like in the presence of the overwhelming mystery of God's ways.

Faith still comes to its limits. Responses can still be fearful. We too are often on the edge of what is humanly possible. 'How can this be?' Now, as then, God is at work. Fear not – and say 'yes'.

'Here am I… let it be with me according to your word.' Amen.

DAVID RUNCORN

Mary

Elizabeth... exclaimed... 'Blessed is she who believed that there would be a fulfilment of what was spoken to her by the Lord.' And Mary said, 'My soul magnifies the Lord... for he has looked with favour on the lowly state of his servant. Surely from now on all generations will call me blessed; for the Mighty One has done great things for me... He has scattered the proud in the imagination of their hearts... brought down the powerful from their thrones and lifted up the lowly... and sent the rich away empty.'

Throughout the Christmas story people, and angels, keep breaking into song. Throughout church history one of the surest signs of spiritual renewal and the inbreaking of God in new ways is the outbreak of worship. Of the songs of Christmas, Mary's is surely the most revolutionary, subversive and astonishing. An unmarried, pregnant village girl bursts into a song that boldly prophecies the overturning of established powers and proclaims the complete reversal of the social order for the rich and the poor alike.

When Mary declares, 'Surely, from now on all generations will call me blessed', she is not boasting or claiming she is God's special favourite. Quite the reverse. Hers is a song of profound humility. She knows that if she, unknown and of no importance or status, is receiving such a blessing from God then a radically new world order is being declared.

She has been called 'the first of the little people'. The first follower in the new kingdom of God's love and justice. She gives voice to the voiceless, a name to the nameless. In the spirit of her song, Luke continues to emphasise the favoured place of the poor, the marginalised and women – all welcomed and given special place in the ministry of Jesus. By contrast the wealthy and powerful find themselves under warning and judgement. Not because they are rich, but because of how they are attached to it – confusing their wealth with importance and divine favour and withholding it from those in need.

Mary is still singing to us. Listen to the music. A new world is coming. Because she is blessed, we are.

May I give voice to the voiceless and share
generously with the poor. Amen.

DAVID RUNCORN

John

Now the time came for Elizabeth to give birth, and she bore a son... On the eighth day they came to circumcise the child, and they were going to name him Zechariah after his father. But his mother said, 'No; he is to be called John'... Then they began motioning to his father to find out what name he wanted to give him. He asked for a writing tablet and wrote, 'His name is John.' And all of them were amazed. Immediately his mouth was opened and his tongue freed, and he began to speak, praising God.

Zechariah has been without hearing or speech for nine months, since the angel imposed it on him in the temple sanctuary. We can hardly imagine what that must have been like to live with, or what journey of faith and understanding he has been on. Someone recently shared their experience of sudden, total hearing loss. It was utterly traumatic and required enormous adjustments. This would have changed every part of Zechariah's life. His public ministry as a priest would have surely come to halt.

Now the baby is born, and he must be circumcised and named. In that society the expectation was that a baby boy would be named after the father. But Elizabeth is faithful to the angel's instruction to Zechariah and insists he will be called John. This story is not following any familiar human tradition or expectation. The boy's name, like his calling, comes from outside human will and planning.

The neighbours assume Elizabeth must have got it wrong. They ask Zechariah. We now glimpse how Zechariah has been communicating all these months. A clay tablet and stick to write with – the ancient version of an iPad. English translations suggest a simple agreement: 'His name is John.' But this does not convey the force of his response in the original Greek: 'John *is his name!*' You sense he is writing with such emphatic conviction he almost breaks the stylus.

Immediately, his voice is restored and what pours out is a torrent of praise. It was a bewildered old priest that went into silence those months before. It is a fiery, passionate prophet that emerges out of it, whose song has been sung by the Christian church ever since.

Lord, teach me the silence that helps your promises go deep in me. Amen.

DAVID RUNCORN

The newborn Jesus

In those days a decree went out from Caesar Augustus that all the world should be registered… Joseph also went… to the city of David called Bethlehem, because he was descended from the house and family of David… with Mary, to whom he was engaged and who was expecting a child. While they were there, the time came for her to deliver her child. And she gave birth to her firstborn son and wrapped him in bands of cloth and laid him in a manger, because there was no place in the guest room.'

'While they were there, the time came…' That means they had been there a while, in what was Joseph's home area. He would have had property and family in the region. In our Christmas nativity plays the action is very compressed. It all happens just in time on Christmas night. Joseph and Mary only just arrive in time and the baby is born with everyone all there at once. The story suggests Mary went into labour while they were in Bethlehem itself and needed somewhere secluded straight away. The inn would certainly have been crowded but not full. But there was no appropriate room for a woman in labour. No one was being unwelcoming. Perhaps it was the innkeeper who arranged for the manger.

Luke tells us the newborn Jesus was wrapped in swaddling clothes and laid in a manger. Swaddling was the custom in those rural communities. A manger was the feeding place at the lower end of the typical one-room houses of that town. This detail is mentioned again when the angels appear to the shepherds and announce Jesus' birth. The shepherds needed some persuading they were to be special guests at the birth of the long-awaited Messiah. 'This will be a sign to you,' says the angel, to reassure them, 'you will find a baby wrapped in cloths and lying in a manger' (Luke 2:12, NIV).

What would they understand this to be a sign of? Surely this is for the important and the significant, not the poor. But this baby is not to be found in a palace. Only the humble and the poor use a manger as a cot. The shepherds would have heard the angel's words and thought: 'He is one of us!'

Thank you for becoming one of us. Amen.

DAVID RUNCORN

Simeon and Anna

When the time came... they brought him up to Jerusalem to present him to the Lord... Now there was a man in Jerusalem whose name was Simeon... Guided by the Spirit, Simeon came into the temple, and when the parents brought in the child Jesus... Simeon took him in his arms and praised God, saying, 'Master, now you are dismissing your servant in peace... for my eyes have seen your salvation'... There was also a prophet, Anna... of a great age... She came and began to praise God.

The moving story of Simeon and Anna meeting the baby Jesus is the central reading of the ancient festival called Candlemas, which falls on 2 February, 40 days after 25 December. It marks the end of the Christmas season and points forward to Lent. By tradition it also provides an ancient weather forecast. The saying goes: 'If Candlemas Day be fair and bright, winter will have another fight. If Candlemas Day brings cloud and rain, winter won't come again.' It comes at the turning of the seasons. Here is the familiar longing for signs of a world turning from the death of winter to the light and life of spring.

This story in the temple is also happening at a turning point. Spiritually, it is the place where old and new faith meet. The young Mary and Joseph bring their baby Jesus to the temple as required by the law. The old Simeon and Anna, who have been faithfully waiting, hoping and longing for their people's faith to come to fulfilment, joyfully recognise this moment as everything their world has been waiting for.

Picture the scene. Young and old face each other. And between them both – the turning point – is the baby Jesus. Simeon holds the child with joy. 'My eyes have seen your salvation', he says.

Here in western Europe, this story finds us today still in the dark of the winter season. But we know those longings for the turning from winter to spring, death to life, darkness to light. May Jesus be our midpoint too, the meeting place of all our longings and the faith for new beginnings. May this story become our own.

Let this be the springtime of your church. Amen.

DAVID RUNCORN

The boy Jesus

Now every year his parents went to Jerusalem for the… Passover… When the festival was ended… the boy Jesus stayed behind in Jerusalem, but his parents were unaware of this… They went a day's journey… When they did not find him, they returned to Jerusalem to search for him. After three days they found him in the temple… His mother said to him, 'Child, why have you treated us like this?'… He said to them, 'Why were you searching for me? Did you not know that I must be in my Father's house?'… His mother treasured all these things in her heart.

It is easy to imagine social media responses to the news that a couple had left a faraway city to return home without knowing their child was not with them. They journeyed for a whole day before realising it! This must have been traumatic for Mary and Joseph, but this is not negligence, actually. Here is a glimpse of life in a secure, close-knit rural community on pilgrimage together, where childcare was a shared responsibility. In the context of our modern concerns about safeguarding and well-being, there is much to notice and admire here, rather than to judge.

Yet Jesus is missing, and it takes three days to find him. His response to Mary's rebuke sounds neither sensitive nor repentant. Not for the first time, Jesus is discovering that realities which for him are totally natural and self-evident are not understood at all by those around him. 'Did you not know?' he asks, apparently in genuine surprise. That was a conversation that surely continued on the journey home.

Luke tells us that Jesus returned to Nazareth and lived in obedience to them, the implication being that he did not do this again. But his true home, his divine parenthood, were briefly revealed in that temple scene. Luke now points us to Mary. He clearly spent time with Mary, and her qualities of careful listening and inward reflection are ones he noticed and draws our attention to. An experience that must have been traumatic and bruising for her is here described as something she deeply treasured. The journey of faith is not always easy, but we too can trust where it leads.

Help my moments of bewilderment to become
sources of treasured faith. Amen.

DAVID RUNCORN

Matthew's Christmas

 Congratulations on making it through another Christmas! I hope that you have managed to engage with the eternal truth which is at the heart of the nativity – the incarnation of God in Christ, born on earth so that he might redeem humanity, providing a lived example of what it is to be a child of God. I hope that amid the wrapping paper, washing up, relatives and general disruption of the daily routine you found an element of peace and of deep joy. I pray that in hearing the familiar story of journeying, arrival and birth you were reconnected once more with your creator in a new and deeper way and that the message of Christmas has found its way into your heart.

This message is at once timeless and eternally new. In my years as a parish priest, I have often felt my heart sink at the thought of finding yet another way of telling the Christmas story, but the miracle is that there is always one to be found. The emphasis may change from year to year, but the arrival of hope can always be celebrated.

This is where the two versions of the Christmas story that we have – in the gospels of Luke and Matthew – are so interesting. We are all aware that the overall Christmas narrative is a combination of everything that Luke and Matthew have to offer – angels speak to Joseph and Mary; the child is established as belonging to the line of David; he is born of the Holy Spirit in Bethlehem. The infant and his family receive visitors, they travel from Bethlehem and he is raised in Nazareth. To these essentials other elements have been added, some based on fact, others not so much – I myself have told the story of the Christmas rabbit, the Christmas mouse and the Christmas snail all visiting the infant Jesus, and I am by no means the most fanciful of storytellers.

But for these four days at the end of the year, we are going to peel apart Matthew's Christmas and explore some of the elements which are his alone, perhaps finding in them a new way to encounter the meaning of the Messiah's birth and its message for the world.

SALLY WELCH

A world shattered

When Herod realised that he had been outwitted by the Magi, he was furious, and he gave orders to kill all the boys in Bethlehem and its vicinity who were two years old and under, in accordance with the time he had learned from the Magi. Then what was said through the prophet Jeremiah was fulfilled: 'A voice is heard in Ramah, weeping and great mourning, Rachel weeping for her children and refusing to be comforted, because they are no more.'

Holy Innocents Day comes crashing into the post-Christmas lull with a devastating blow. Into the midst of adults just starting back at work or beginning those chores and activities that the festivities had postponed, while children are still dazed from too much sugar and too many unfamiliar relatives, blasts this tale of outrageous cruelty, an event which must have devastated the small community of Bethlehem, destroying expectations for the future, shattering the hopes and dreams of so many families.

Why is it included here? Why does Matthew include it at all? Perhaps to show that the way of Christ will not be all bright stars and angels, that those who announce the truth must expect opposition, that all who speak of a different way will face a hostile reaction from the world. For us it is a reminder that not all Christmas Days will be tinsel-strewn merriment, stuffed with good food and celebration. Those of us who are fortunate enough to be able to celebrate should make space to pray for others whose life path has not led that way. We should remember those who spend Christmas alone or who are suffering or dying. We must hold in our hearts those for whom Christmas is emptier of people than it was before, for whom celebrations hold a hollow echo of loved ones seen no longer.

But we must remember also that 'the light shines in the darkness, and the darkness has not overcome it' (John 1:5). And we must hold on to hope, even as the tears stream down our faces.

'Yet in thy dark streets shineth the everlasting light; the hopes and fears of all the years are met in thee tonight' (Phillips Brooks, 1835–93).

SALLY WELCH

The family tree

This is the genealogy of Jesus the Messiah the son of David, the son of Abraham: Abraham was the father of Isaac, Isaac the father of Jacob, Jacob the father of Judah and his brothers, Judah the father of Perez and Zerah, whose mother was Tamar, Perez the father of Hezron, Hezron the father of Ram, Ram the father of Amminadab, Amminadab the father of Nahshon, Nahshon the father of Salmon, Salmon the father of Boaz, whose mother was Rahab, Boaz the father of Obed, whose mother was Ruth, Obed the father of Jesse, and Jesse the father of King David.

What a glorious roll-call of names – some familiar, such as Jacob, Boaz and Jesse; others whose names will appear only once in the Bible and might never be remembered except by dedicated biblical scholars. These first verses firmly root the birth of Christ into the story of the children of Israel.

Jesus is the Messiah; he is a member of the family of David, whose history can be traced right back to the first covenant God made with Abraham, the promise that his offspring would be as numerous as the stars in the sky and as the sand on the seashore (Genesis 22:17). Jesus is of royal descent, which is fortunate as he will be going head to head with kings and rulers, demonstrating a different kind of leadership, a subversive type of power, one which undermines the traditional worldly attributes of strength, wealth and success.

We are reminded of the exodus and the exile, events which shaped the people of Israel, happenings which find their resolution not in an earthly place but in the person of Christ. We note the presence of women who were not of the house of Israel – Tamar, Rahab, Ruth and Uriah's wife – who highlight the nature of the gospel as a gift for all nations, with all people invited to become children of God.

These opening verses are a deep-breathed poem which lands with an earth-changing thump on 'Jesus who is called the Messiah' (v. 16) – the springboard for the miraculous happenings which will be unfolded in the rest of the gospel.

'O come, O Key of David, come and open wide our heavenly home'
(John Mason Neale, 1818–66).

SALLY WELCH

A righteous man

When his mother Mary had been engaged to Joseph, but before they lived together, she was found to be pregnant from the Holy Spirit. Her husband Joseph, being a righteous man and unwilling to expose her to public disgrace, planned to divorce her quietly. But just when he had resolved to do this, an angel of the Lord appeared to him in a dream and said, 'Joseph, son of David, do not be afraid to take Mary as your wife, for the child conceived in her is from the Holy Spirit. She will bear a son, and you are to name him Jesus, for he will save his people from their sins.'

The King James Bible translation of this passage describes Joseph as a 'just' man; the New International Version as 'faithful to the law', while the contemporary translation *The Message* calls him 'chagrined but noble'. All these imply someone who is perhaps a stickler for the rules, who knows his place in the order of the world, who has a strong sense of what is right and proper. Perhaps also there is a sense of someone who might honour the letter of the law rather than the more forgiving spirit; a hint of smugness, of self-righteousness even.

Certainly Joseph's initial reaction to Mary's pregnancy is all that it should be according to the code of the day – obviously he was not going to marry her, but nor was he going to disgrace her. The plan was simply to send her quietly back to her family and pretend the engagement never happened.

But then Joseph dreams. It must have been strange and troubling, that dream. And what courage it must have taken to base the rest of your life on a dream! Joseph's planned future, which has already received a knock from Mary, is turned on its head again. He must take on the care of this special child and his mother, support them and protect them against the words of the world. He must set aside his own needs and wishes and, were he to know it or not, face difficulty and danger in the early years of escape and hiding.

And so a new definition of 'righteous', 'faithful', 'just' and 'noble' is born.

'As Joseph was a-walking, he heard an angel sing, this night shall be the birthday of Christ, the heav'nly King' (Henry John Gauntlett, 1805–76).

SALLY WELCH

Herod's disturbance

After Jesus was born in Bethlehem in Judea, during the time of King Herod, Magi from the east came to Jerusalem and asked, 'Where is the one who has been born king of the Jews? We saw his star when it rose and have come to worship him.' When King Herod heard this he was disturbed, and all Jerusalem with him.

The wise men must have arrived at Herod's palace full of excitement and joy. But even in their arrival they are setting off a train of circumstances which spell disaster not only for Jesus but also for the community which shelters his birth. Herod, ruler of an occupied country, sitting uncertainly on an unstable throne, held in power by the authority of the Romans, is informed that the king of the Jews has been born. A direct threat faces Herod, and he is afraid.

And not just him, but 'all Jerusalem with him'. For what sort of instability and disruption will this 'king' sow, threatening the *status quo* and all who have a vested interest in it? Herod and his officials react with fear, which soon degenerates into violence, and the order of slaughter is made.

How saddened must the Magi have been, deceived by Herod's apparent eagerness to discover the whereabouts of the child, fondly thinking that he shared their delight and joy, only to learn from an angel of the disaster they had triggered by their arrival and unthinking announcement. They are not to blame, but they and others must face the consequences. The Magi return to their countries 'by another route' (v. 12), and while the holy family finds safety in Egypt, not everyone is so lucky, and a community is plunged into the terror of death.

How do we react to the mixture that is Matthew's Christmas story? With gratitude for the 'righteousness' of Joseph; awe at God's great plans for humanity evidenced in his promise to Abraham 'and his seed'; sorrow for the brokenness of the world and the cruelty of individuals; and joy with the magi, who offer their gifts to the king who brings hope to the world.

'Joy to the world, the Lord is come! Let earth receive her king'
(Isaac Watts, 1674–1748).

SALLY WELCH

I would like to make a donation to support BRF Ministries.
Please use my gift for:

☐ Where the need is greatest   ☐ Anna Chaplaincy   ☐ Living Faith

☐ Messy Church   ☐ Parenting for Faith

Title	First name/initials	Surname

Address		

	Postcode

Email

Telephone

Signature	Date

Please accept my gift of:

☐ £2   ☐ £5   ☐ £10   ☐ £20   Other £ [   ]

by (*delete as appropriate*):

☐ Cheque/Charity Voucher payable to 'BRF'

☐ MasterCard/Visa/Debit card/Charity card

Name on card

Card no. ☐☐☐☐ ☐☐☐☐ ☐☐☐☐ ☐☐☐☐

Expires end [M M] [Y Y]   Security code* [☐☐☐]   *Last 3 digits on the reverse of the card

Signature	Date

Please complete other side of form ➡

141

BRF Ministries Gift Aid Declaration

In order to Gift Aid your donation, you must tick the box below.

☐ I want to Gift Aid my donation and any donation I make in the future or have made in the past four years to BRF Ministries

I am a UK taxpayer and understand that if I pay less Income Tax and/or Capital Gains Tax in the current tax year than the amount of Gift Aid claimed on all my donations, it is my responsibility to pay any difference.

Please notify BRF Ministries if you want to cancel this Gift Aid declaration, change your name or home address, or no longer pay sufficient tax on your income and/or capital gains.

You can also give online at **brf.org.uk/donate**, which reduces our administration costs, making your donation go further.

Our ministry is only possible because of the generous support of individuals, churches, trusts and gifts in wills.

☐ I would like to leave a gift to BRF Ministries in my will.
Please send me further information.

☐ I would like to find out about giving a regular gift to BRF Ministries.

For help or advice regarding making a gift, please contact our fundraising team +44 (0)1235 462305

Your privacy

We will use your personal data to process this transaction. From time to time we may send you information about the work of BRF Ministries that we think may be of interest to you. Our privacy policy is available at **brf.org.uk/privacy**. Please contact us if you wish to discuss your mailing preferences.

Registered with

FR

FUNDRAISING
REGULATOR

← Please complete other side of form

Please return this form to 'Freepost BRF'
No other address information or stamp is needed

BRF

Bible Reading Fellowship is a charity (233280) and company limited by guarantee (301324), registered in England and Wales

Reading New Daylight in a group

GORDON GILES

It is good to talk. While the Rule of Benedict, which formed the spiritual foundations of so many ecclesiastical foundations, recommended daily scripture reading as a key aspect of the community life of work and prayer, during Lent especially each monk was allocated a book to read daily. Benedict's monks did not talk much, but nowadays discussion and reflection can be helpful and enlightening when reading passages that others are simultaneously also reading. Separated by space, as each reads alone, we are yet connected by the common food of scripture, taken in our own time at our own pace. We each chew on it in our own way, and we can all learn from each other's insights and interpretations. To assist with that, here are some open questions that may enable discussion in a Bible study or other group who gather to take further what is published here. The same questions may also aid personal devotion too. Use them as you wish, and may God bless you on your journey as you read, mark and inwardly digest holy words to ponder and nourish the soul

General discussion starters

These can be used for any study series within this issue. There are no right or wrong answers; these questions are simply to enable conversation.

- What do you think is the main idea or theme of the author in this series? Did that come across strongly?

- Have any of the issues discussed touched on personal – or shared – aspects of your life?

- What evidence or stories do the authors draw on to illuminate, or be illuminated by, the passages of scripture.

- Which do you prefer: scripture informing daily modern life or modern life shining a new light on scripture?

- Does the author call you to action in a realistic and achievable way? Do you think their ideas will work in the secular world?

- Have any specific passages struck you personally? If so, how and why? Is God speaking to you through scripture and reflection?

- Was anything completely new to you? Any 'eureka' or jaw-dropping moments? If so, what difference will that make?

Questions for discussion

Colossians (Jane Walters)

- In chapter 1, in what ways does Paul encourage, provoke and challenge our prayer habits?
- How can we rebut the argument that all religions are equal and each pathway to God a valid one?
- What are some of our culture's 'hollow and deceptive philosophies' (see Colossians 2:8, NIV) that we must guard against?
- If we have taken off the 'old self' (Colossians 3:9, NIV) and put on the new, why is it that we still sin?
- St Francis of Assisi reputedly said, 'Preach the gospel at all times; if necessary, use words.' How does this square with Paul's teaching here? (4:6)
- Are there people in your church or elsewhere who are currently supporting you or have made an impact on your life? How can you best convey your appreciation of them?

Jonah, the reluctant prophet (Amanda Bloor)

- Think of a time when a task was put before you that seemed impossible for you to complete. What did you do? On reflection, would you approach the same task differently now?
- Do you have a prayer that you can reach for in times of trouble? The Lord's Prayer is an obvious example, but there are many others. Try learning a new prayer and committing it to memory so that it is always with you.
- How do you think that Jonah felt when the sailors were blaming him for the storm? If you were on the boat with him, what would you advise him to do?
- Can you remember a moment when things felt very dark, but something or someone brought light and hope? What might that say about God's presence in our lives?
- Reflect upon your usual daily schedule. Where might you carve out a little time and space to find quiet in order to focus upon God? What is it that you find helpful when listening for God's voice?

- When things don't go as expected, or if your attempts to do as God asks fall flat, what might give you encouragement?
- What are the barriers that prevent us – as individuals and as a community – from responding generously to others? How might they be overcome?

Matthew's Advent (Paul Gravelle)

- We are going through a period of unusual natural and man-made disasters. Do you think these are signs of the end?
- Would you say that the spread of evil is increasing in the world? If so, what examples can you give?
- 'Wherever there is a dead body, the vultures will gather' (Matthew 24:28, GNT). Jesus said this about false messiahs. What do you make of it?
- Do you think Jesus' promise to the dying thief applies to all believers. If so, how? If not, why not?
- Many Christians believe they will be 'raptured' to escape persecution. Can you see this anywhere in Jesus's words as recorded in Matthew 24:29–31?

Meet the author: Catherine Williams

How did you come to faith and what were the earliest influences on your Christian journey?

Despite not growing up in a Christian family, I was a very spiritual child, who loved the natural world and had a vivid imagination. I was fascinated by the stories of Jesus that were taught at school and often imagined walking alongside him. Aged seven I joined the Brownies so I could go to church parade! At the age of twelve, I joined a church choir, attended church regularly on my own and was lovingly nurtured by the Christian community. Baptised and confirmed as a teenager, I studied theology at university, married a priest and was later ordained. All this time I was strolling with Jesus, aware of the Holy Spirit working in both me and the world around me. My conversion is ongoing as I slowly become who God is calling me to be. God's adventures are full of surprises, so commitment and recommitment happen regularly!

Tell us about where you live, your church context and ministry.

I live on a country estate close to the beautiful north Norfolk coast, where my husband is incumbent to six rural churches. There's a forest on my door-step and beaches close by. I enjoy walking among the trees and watching the birds on the salt marshes. Having worked in vocational discernment at parish, diocesan and national levels, my main ministry is now as a spiritual director, retreat leader and preacher. I also write, edit and record a variety of spiritual resources for the Christian community in the UK and beyond. This spacious ministry requires plenty of prayer and reflection, and I am becoming increasingly contemplative. Much of the ministry I undertake is hidden and very few realise the extent of it. I like it that way!

What is your favourite book of the Bible and why?

Song of Songs. This always raises a few eyebrows! I love the passionate intimacy described in it, which nourishes my relationship with Jesus, the divine lover. It's not much in fashion these days, but Song of Songs has been hugely influential down the centuries, and there are some wonderful reflections, sermons, poems and music written by scholars and mystics waiting to be explored. On the first day of every month, I have a Song of Songs day, when I read the text, study the medieval material and recommit to walking closely with Jesus. I pray through the tasks and potential encounters of the month ahead listening for the Holy Spirit as she leads and guides. This monthly spiritual practice keeps me rooted and on track with God.

If you could advise a younger generation, what would you say to them?

First, I wouldn't advise; I'd start by listening. I'm often inspired by my young adult children and their friends. They are wise and passionate people, full of life and very committed to justice and equity concerns, both for humanity and the planet. I sense God is mightily at work in these young lives even when not acknowledged. We have much to learn from them. I think my one piece of advice for all of us, whatever our age or stage of life, would be from the fourteenth-century Italian mystic Catherine of Siena: 'Be who God meant you to be and you will set the world on fire.'

Recommended reading

The lectionary readings for Advent speak of making a straight path towards God, but many of us find our own route decidedly winding. Biblical characters in the story of the incarnation are called to set out on the road to discipleship using any means of carriage they can.

BRF Ministries' Advent book for 2025, *Donkey Roads and Camel Treks* by Gemma Simmonds, offers user-friendly encouragement (with the occasional spur onwards) to explore what helps and what hinders us in this journey to deeper encounter with the flesh-and-blood God whom we find in scripture, in our lived experience and in the least of his sisters and brothers.

The following is an edited version of the introduction.

I tend to approach Advent with mixed feelings. It is my favourite liturgical season, and I usually begin to feel a delightful sense of anticipation somewhere in mid-October. But as my time is ruled by the academic term, I also approach it with a certain dread. The beginning of December and the weeks that follow are among the busiest of the year, and I know before I have started that I am likely to miss out on the riches of the readings, antiphons, carols and prayers because I have so little time to stop and relish them. There's always something of a sense of opportunity missed, of time ill spent and of invitation not fully enjoyed and celebrated.

My sense of anticipation before Christmas is also countered by the knowledge that Advent and Christmas are not universally part of everyone's feel-good factor. Many find that Christmas increases any sense of loss or isolation they may already be feeling. Domestic violence always goes up over the Christmas period as families have more time together. Where alcohol, pent-up tensions and simmering anger are in close proximity, this can turn into a powder keg of violence that can explode at any time.

Consumer pressure also pushes debt up within families when it's believed that love is proved by spending, so that parents feel obliged to spend money they don't have on presents their children don't need. This consumer pressure fills me with feelings of outrage when I begin to see mince pies, Christmas puddings and Advent calendars on supermarket shelves in September.

For me, at best, times and seasons are welcome opportunities for marking the wonderful variety and rhythms of the year. When they are hijacked, by-passed or ridden roughshod over by the demands of consumer consciousness gone mad, it fills me with disgust. I post enraged photographs of these ill-timed items on WhatsApp and Facebook and make Grumpy Old Woman comments to my patient friends, while ranting about the pointlessness of so-called Advent calendars, which, instead of being a means of increasing anticipation of Christmas through delayed gratification, are simply another excuse to turn the season into a bloated consumer fest.

I have a sense of God rolling divine eyes at me every year. 'Not on about that again, are you? Do you still not understand that I'm willing to take anything I can get on the part of humanity, even if it's the barest remnants of Christian folk memory?' The fourteenth-century English mystic Julian of Norwich claimed remarkably that God is grateful when we remember him. This seems a shocking thing to assert. It sounds as if God is somehow content to take the crumbs off our table. Surely that can't be true?

Yet we have ample evidence from the words and behaviour of Jesus, the Word made flesh, that this is exactly how God is with us. He takes the clumsy faith of a tax collector hidden up a tree, the reticent hope of a Roman centurion unsure of his welcome, the thanks of the one grateful leper and the despairing prayers of a woman outcast and shamed by her defiling illness, and transforms them into life-changing gifts of grace. Prayer and faith are never performance-related activities, nor are they things that we do for God. They are in themselves gifts that God gives and does for us.

We may think that our own or other people's approach to Christmas covers the bare minimum, but the Christmas story, as it unfolds, is all about God's lavish generosity encountering the meagreness of our poverty and transforming it into gift.

Most of the characters in official positions are gloriously unaware of their own limitations. Think of Zechariah, Herod, Caesar Augustus and even the Magi. They are all men of power, but they have no idea or fail to recognise what is happening right beneath their noses. Mary and Elizabeth, Joseph and the shepherds manage rather better, but, like the Magi, each of them also has to undertake a journey that consists in relinquishing set notions of who God is and how God acts in human affairs, accepting that, in this case, they are dealing with the God of surprises.

In Nativity plays and Christmas liturgies where real sheep and donkeys appear, they are usually clean, well-behaved, soft-pelted and enchanting.

My own experience of riding a donkey or a camel for any length of time is an entirely different matter. During a sabbatical visit to the Holy Land in 2019, I had the great privilege of spending a term at the Tantur Institute, which stands above the checkpoint into Bethlehem. We travelled to St Catherine's Monastery in the Sinai desert and were offered the opportunity to trek up the mountain and watch the sunrise.

It seemed a wonderful idea at the time, but I knew my physical limits, so I agreed to ride up the mountain on a camel. I don't think I have ever had a more agonisingly uncomfortable journey, well-padded in the rear though I am. I don't know if, like T.S. Eliot's camels in 'The Journey of the Magi', they were galled and sore-footed, but they were certainly refractory. I came to have a healthy respect for the Magi themselves and an equal respect and sympathy for the heavily pregnant Mary journeying from Nazareth to Bethlehem on her donkey.

It all looks so calm and beautiful on the Christmas cards, but the reality is far harder, more uncomfortable, tedious and painful. I suspect that Advent and Christmas themselves are rather like this for many people. We love the idea, but getting down to it can be daunting for all sorts of reasons. Family dynamics can be tense, financial or social challenges can make what we offer seem paltry in light of the yearly expanding Christmas extravaganza pressed on us by the advertising industry. We want to exhibit faith, hope and love, but they can all waver before the bitter realities on the daily news.

Yet I remember a moment, halfway up Mount Sinai, when we got off our camels with distinct relief and crowded into a little bivouac where local people plied us with herbal tea and vastly overpriced snacks. It was so cold that we shivered even though we were packed in like sardines, but there was a real sense of communion and of fellowship as we snatched a few minutes of comfort from one another while the camels groaned and snorted on their knees on the edge of the mountain outside.

My hope is that these reflections might be of use not only for individuals once more setting out on the yearly road to Bethlehem, but also for groups journeying together in the global caravan of half-believers, dogged hopers and random fellow travellers.

The themes behind the Christmas story have never seemed as relevant as they do at the time of writing.

The political regime in the United States triumphed at the polls with an anti-migrant, us-and-them rhetoric which has distinct echoes of the refusal of hospitality at the inn of Bethlehem.

Legislation that would make it easier to kill the unborn, the terminally ill, the frail elderly and the disabled sits uncomfortably well within the story of Herod and his massacre of the innocents, as do the disastrous wars currently raging between Israel and Palestine, Russia and Ukraine, and in Sudan, Myanmar, Yemen and beyond.

The failure of many religious leaders to listen to critical questions and to the voice of experience among the faithful is akin to the perturbation felt by 'the whole of Jerusalem' as those on the outside arrive with a message from God whose implications overturn all the comfortable assumptions of those on the inside about how God acts within the world and how religious systems should function.

Once again, in our own time, it is the poor, the disregarded and the dispossessed who so often see more clearly than those in power, both secular and sacred, whose privilege can blunt their capacity to see things as they are and imagine how they could be.

Here and now, this Advent, we are invited to saddle up our camels or our donkeys and begin the journey anew. Even if we only get to spend a few minutes a day or a few snatched moments during the general Advent mayhem, God is more generous than we could ever ask or imagine. The scriptures, songs and themes of Advent and Christmas are so rich that we cannot escape being reminded that if we give God a millimetre, then a mile will be taken. Jesus, who fed 5,000 with a few loaves and two fish, will take what crumbs of faith, hope and love we can gather and will make a feast of them.

That's why it's worth setting out with our companions and becoming Advent pilgrims in whatever way we can.

To order a copy of this book, please use the order form or visit **brfonline.org.uk**

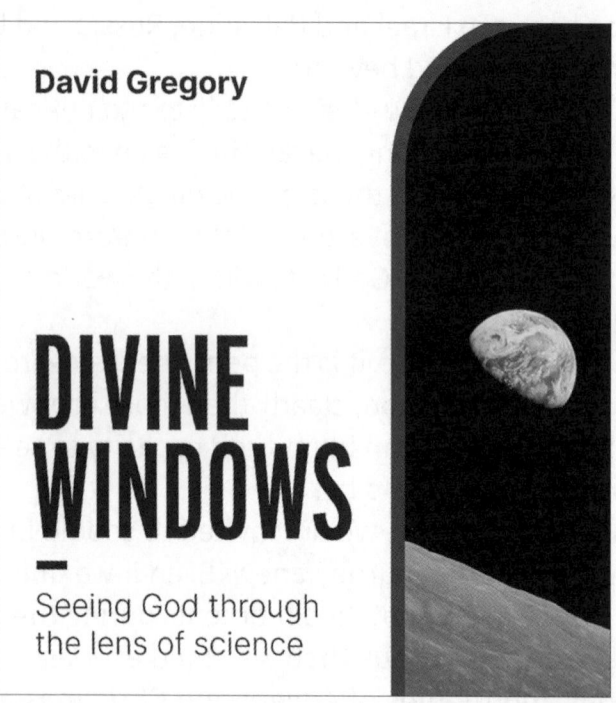

Dive into *Divine Windows*, where science and faith meet. Explore nature and science imagery with wonder, play and communion. See God's creative hand in the world around us through a fresh lens. Through reflective commentary and an inspiring series of nature and science imagery, scientist David Gregory shows how scientific beauty and discovery go hand in hand with the shaping of creation by a higher purpose.

Divine Windows
Seeing God through the lens of science
David Gregory

978 1 80039 331 8 £12.99
brfonline.org.uk

To order

Online: **brfonline.org.uk**
Telephone: +44 (0)1865 319700
Mon–Fri 9.30–17.00

Delivery times within the UK are normally 15 working days. Prices are correct at the time of going to press but may change without prior notice.

Title	Price	Qty	Total
Donkey Roads and Camel Treks	£9.99		
Divine Windows	£12.99		

POSTAGE AND PACKING CHARGES			
Order value	UK	Europe	Rest of world
Under £7.00	£2.00	Available on request	Available on request
£7.00–£29.99	£3.00		
£30.00 and over	FREE		

Total value of books	
Postage and packing	
Donation*	
Total for this order	

* Please complete and return the Gift Aid declaration on page 142.

Please complete in BLOCK CAPITALS

Title _____ First name/initials _____ Surname _____

Address _____

_____ Postcode _____

Acc. No. _____ Telephone _____

Email _____

Method of payment

☐ Cheque (made payable to BRF) ☐ MasterCard / Visa

Card no. ☐☐☐☐ ☐☐☐☐ ☐☐☐☐ ☐☐☐☐ ☐☐☐☐

Expires end [M][M] [Y][Y] Security code ☐☐☐ Last 3 digits on the reverse of the card

Please return this form to:

BRF Ministries, 15 The Chambers, Vineyard, Abingdon OX14 3FE | **enquiries@brf.org.uk**
For terms and cancellation information, please visit **brfonline.org.uk/terms**.

Bible Reading Fellowship (BRF) is a charity (233280) and company limited by guarantee (301324), registered in England and Wales

BRF Ministries needs you!

If you're one of our many thousands of regular *New Daylight* readers you will know all about the rich rewards of regular Bible reading and the value of daily notes to guide, inform and inspire you. Here are some recent comments from *New Daylight* readers:

> 'Thank you for all the many inspiring writings that help so much when things are tough.'

> 'Just right for me – I learned a lot!'

> 'We looked forward to each day's message as we pondered each passage and comment.'

If you have similarly positive things to say about *New Daylight*, would you be willing to help spread the word about these popular resources? Could you follow the example of long-standing *New Daylight* reader Beryl Fudge and form a *New Daylight* reading group, not to take the place of private prayer and reading but to share insights and deepen understanding. 'I've quite a few friends who also take the notes and we discuss them in the group,' says Beryl: '... there's so much in them every day. What I most value in *New Daylight* is the way that they connect the Old and New Testament scriptures with what's happening here and now.'

It doesn't need to be complicated: every issue of *New Daylight* includes questions for reflection or discussion.

We can supply further information if you need it and would love to hear about it if you do form a *New Daylight* reading group.

For more information:

- Email **enquiries@brf.org.uk**
- Phone us on **+44 (0)1865 319700** Mon–Fri 9.30–17.00
- Write to us at BRF Ministries, 15 The Chambers, Vineyard, Abingdon OX14 3FE

Inspiring people of all ages to grow in Christian faith

At BRF Ministries, we long for people of all ages to grow in faith and understanding of the Bible. That's what all our work as a charity is about.

- Our **Living Faith** range of resources helps Christians go deeper in their understanding of scripture, in prayer and in their walk with God. Our conferences and events bring people together to share this journey, while our Holy Habits resources help whole congregations grow together as disciples of Jesus, living out and sharing their faith.

- We also want to make it easier for local churches to engage effectively in ministry and mission – by helping them bring new families into a growing relationship with God through **Messy Church** or by supporting churches as they nurture the spiritual life of older people through **Anna Chaplaincy**.

- Our **Parenting for Faith** team coaches parents and others to raise God-connected children and teens, and enables churches to fully support them.

Do you share our vision?

Though a significant proportion of BRF Ministries' funding is generated through our charitable activities, we are dependent on the generous support of individuals, churches and charitable trusts.

If you share our vision, would you help us to enable even more people of all ages to grow in faith? Your prayers and financial support are vital for the work that we do. You could:

- support us with a regular donation or one-off gift
- consider leaving a gift to BRF Ministries in your will
- encourage your church to support us as part of your church's giving to home mission – perhaps focusing on a specific ministry or programme
- most important of all, support us with your prayers.

Donate at **brf.org.uk/donate** or use the form on pages 141–42.

Everything has its time

For everything there is a season, and a time for every matter under heaven.
ECCLESIASTES 3:1 (NRSV)

These four months seem to cover many seasons, as we start back after the summer break and move from harvest to autumn, Advent and Christmas, and at BRF Ministries we produce resources from all our ministry teams for all these seasons in turn.

Our resources include books, greetings cards, podcasts, a wide range of training opportunities, Facebook Live sessions, the occasional webinar, and meet-ups, both in person and online. They focus on Anna Chaplaincy, Living Faith, Messy Church and Parenting for Faith, but at the heart we are all BRF Ministries, playing our part in our mission to inspire people of all ages to grow in Christian faith.

To find out about all of the exciting things we are doing, visit our website **brf.org.uk**. From there you can find out about us as a charity and follow links to the ministry websites, and the big red buttons at the top of the page take you straight to our web store and our donations page.

In order to produce these resources and events we are entirely dependent on donations from individuals, churches, charitable trusts and gifts in wills. Every donation is important to us and we are deeply grateful for your continued generosity. If you would like to support us now and in the future, you can become a Friend of BRF Ministries by making a monthly gift of £2 or more – we thank you for your friendship.

Find out more at **brf.org.uk/donate** or get in touch with us on **01235 462305** or via **giving@brf.org.uk**.

The fundraising team at BRF Ministries

Give. Pray. Get involved.
brf.org.uk

NEW DAYLIGHT SUBSCRIPTION RATES

Please note our new subscription rates, current until 30 April 2026:

Individual subscriptions
covering 3 issues for under 5 copies, payable in advance
(including postage & packing):

	UK	Europe	Rest of world
New Daylight	£21.30	£29.55	£35.25
New Daylight Deluxe per set of 3 issues p.a.	£26.55	£36.00	£44.10

Group subscriptions
covering 3 issues for 5 copies or more, sent to one UK address (post free):

New Daylight	£15.75 per set of 3 issues p.a.
New Daylight Deluxe	£19.50 per set of 3 issues p.a.

Please note that the annual billing period for group subscriptions runs from 1 May to 30 April.

Overseas group subscription rates
Available on request. Please email **enquiries@brf.org.uk**.

Copies may also be obtained from Christian bookshops:

New Daylight	£5.25 per copy
New Daylight Deluxe	£6.50 per copy

> All our Bible reading notes can be ordered online
> by visiting **brfonline.org.uk/subscriptions**

NEW DAYLIGHT INDIVIDUAL SUBSCRIPTION FORM

> To set up a recurring subscription, please go to
> **brfonline.org.uk/new-daylight**

Title _____ First name/initials _____ Surname _____

Address _____

_____ Postcode _____

Telephone _____ Email _____

Please send *New Daylight* beginning with the January 2026 / May 2026 / September 2026 issue (*delete as appropriate*):

(*please tick box*)	UK	Europe	Rest of world
New Daylight	☐ £21.30	☐ £29.55	☐ £35.25
New Daylight Deluxe	☐ £26.55	☐ £36.00	☐ £44.10

Optional donation to support the work of BRF Ministries £ _____

Total enclosed £ _____ (cheques should be made payable to 'BRF')

Please complete and return the Gift Aid declaration on page 142 to make your donation even more valuable to us.

Please charge my MasterCard / Visa with £ _____

Card no. ☐☐☐☐ ☐☐☐☐ ☐☐☐☐ ☐☐☐☐

Expires end ☐☐ ☐☐   Security code ☐☐☐   Last 3 digits on the reverse of the card

We will use your personal data to process this order. From time to time we may send you information about the work of BRF Ministries. Please contact us if you wish to discuss your mailing preferences. Our privacy policy is available at **brf.org.uk/privacy**.

Please return this form with the appropriate payment to:
BRF Ministries, 15 The Chambers, Vineyard, Abingdon OX14 3FE
For terms and cancellation information, please visit **brfonline.org.uk/terms**.

Bible Reading Fellowship is a charity (233280) and company limited by guarantee (301324), registered in England and Wales

ND0325

NEW DAYLIGHT GIFT SUBSCRIPTION FORM

☐ I would like to give a gift subscription (please provide both names and addresses):

Title .... First name/initials .... Surname ----------------------------------

Address ---

--- Postcode ----------------------

Telephone ---------------------------- Email --------------------------------------

Gift subscription name --

Gift subscription address --

-- Postcode ----------------------

Gift message (20 words max. or include your own gift card):

Please send *New Daylight* beginning with the January 2026 / May 2026 / September 2026 issue (*delete as appropriate*):

(*please tick box*)	UK	Europe	Rest of world
New Daylight	☐ £21.30	☐ £29.55	☐ £35.25
New Daylight Deluxe	☐ £26.55	☐ £36.00	☐ £44.10

Optional donation to support the work of BRF Ministries £ --------------------

Total enclosed £ ------------------- (cheques should be made payable to 'BRF')

Please complete and return the Gift Aid declaration on page 142 to make your donation even more valuable to us.

Please charge my MasterCard / Visa with £ ------------------

Card no. ☐☐☐☐ ☐☐☐☐ ☐☐☐☐ ☐☐☐☐

Expires end ☐☐ ☐☐ Security code ☐☐ Last 3 digits on the reverse of the card

We will use your personal data to process this order. From time to time we may send you information about the work of BRF Ministries. Please contact us if you wish to discuss your mailing preferences. Our privacy policy is available at **brf.org.uk/privacy**.

Please return this form with the appropriate payment to:
BRF Ministries, 15 The Chambers, Vineyard, Abingdon OX14 3FE
For terms and cancellation information, please visit **brfonline.org.uk/terms**.

Bible Reading Fellowship is a charity (233280) and company limited by guarantee (301324), registered in England and Wales

Ministries

Inspiring people of all ages to grow in Christian faith

BRF Ministries is the
home of Anna Chaplaincy,
Living Faith, Messy Church
and Parenting for Faith

As a charity, our work would not be possible without
fundraising and gifts in wills.
To find out more and to donate,
visit brf.org.uk/give or call +44 (0)1235 462305

Registered with
FUNDRAISING
REGULATOR